T H E   B O O K   O F

Chocolates
&
Petits Fours

T H E   B O O K   O F

Chocolates & Petits Fours

BEVERLEY SUTHERLAND SMITH

Photography by
PHILIP WYMANT

HPBooks®

ANOTHER BEST SELLING VOLUME FROM HP BOOKS®

Published by HP Books® P.O. Box 5367, Tucson, AZ 85703   602/888–2150
ISBN: 0–89586–481–9
Library of Congress Card Number: 86–81045
1st Printing

By arrangement with Salamander Books Ltd. and Merehurst Press, London.

Publisher: Rick Bailey
Editorial Director: Elaine Woodard
Editors: Patricia Aaron, Susan Tomnay, Chris Fayers
Designers: Susan Kinealy, Roger Daniels, Richard Slater, Stuart Willard
Food stylist: Beverley Sutherland Smith
Photographer: Philip Wymant
Typeset by Lineage
Color separation by Fotographics Ltd, London–Hong Kong
Printed by New Interlitho S.p.A., Milan

Contents

Introduction

Petits fours are tiny cookies and iced cakes served at the end of a meal usually with a cup of coffee. One of the greatest French chefs of the eighteenth century, Careme, said that these little cakes were baked in the oven after the large cakes had been removed and the oven had cooled slightly. These after dinner delights extend now to include small fancy cookies, tiny tarts and confectionery, such as chocolate coated fruits, marzipan sweets and nut confections. There has also been an increase of interest in exquisitely molded chocolates to serve after dinner, but there is an added charm in the individual texture and taste which shows in produce which is homemade, even if not as perfect as commercial in appearance. This book has a wide collection of chocolates, petits fours and other confections which I think are especially delicious and vary from those which can be made very quickly to others requiring more time for special occasions. When assembling this collection, I felt it really important that they could be made without the necessity of sweetmaking or chocolate equipment, such as molds, and were not beyond the ability of most home cooks. Not only can these be served after dinner, but many of them make ideal gifts. They are all delicious – the ultimate indulgence after a meal.

Fruity Chocolates

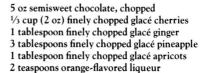

5 oz semisweet chocolate, chopped
⅓ cup (2 oz) finely chopped glacé cherries
1 tablespoon finely chopped glacé ginger
3 tablespoons finely chopped glacé pineapple
1 tablespoon finely chopped glacé apricots
2 teaspoons orange-flavored liqueur

TO DECORATE: 24 almond pieces

Melt 3 oz chocolate in a bowl or top of a double boiler set over pan of simmering water. Drop 24 small chocolate rounds by teaspoon on waxed paper and flatten. Let set.

Mix fruit with liqueur. Let stand for 30 minutes. Using about ½ tablespoon, form fruit mixture into small balls and press to same diameter as chocolate rounds. Place flattened fruit on top of each chocolate round.

To decorate, melt remaining 2 oz chocolate in a bowl or top of a double boiler set over a pan of simmering water. Spoon chocolate into a small pastry bag fitted with a small plain writing tip. Pipe a lattice design on top of each fruity chocolate. Place an almond flake on top of each fruity chocolate. Let set. Store layered with waxed paper, in an airtight container up to 3 weeks.

Makes 24 chocolates.

Chocolate Fruit Crisps

4 oz semisweet chocolate, chopped
¾ cup pitted dates, finely chopped
½ cup pecans, finely chopped
⅓ cup (3 oz) superfine sugar
⅓ cup butter
1 cup (1 oz) rice breakfast cereal
½ cup (1½ oz) shredded coconut

Line a 11″ x 7″ baking pan with foil; grease foil. Melt chocolate in a bowl or top of a double boiler set over a pan of simmering water. Stir until smooth. Spread over foil. Let chocolate partially set.

Heat dates, nuts, sugar and butter in a small saucepan until the butter is hot. Stir occasionally. Combine rice cereal and coconut in a large bowl. Stir in date mixture. Mix well. Spread on top of chocolate base. Spread and flatten mixture firmly so it holds together.

Chill until set. Invert and remove foil. Invert again so rice topping is uppermost. Cut what is needed into strips. Cover and store remainder in refrigerator up to 1 week.

Makes 40 pieces.

Chocolate-Coated Fruit

4 glacé pineapple halves
8 dried apricots
3 large glacé apricots or dried figs
7 oz milk or semisweet chocolate
2 teaspoons unflavored vegetable oil

If dried apricots are very hard, cover with boiling water for 30 seconds. Drain well and pat dry with paper towels. Melt chocolate and oil in a bowl or top of a double boiler set over a pan of simmering water. Stir until smooth.

Dip fruit in chocolate. Hold above bowl to allow excess chocolate to drip away and place on waxed paper.

When cool, refrigerate in a covered container up to 2 weeks. Cut into pieces to expose a cross-section of color, if desired.

Makes 15 pieces.

Dried Fruit Confections

⅓ cup dried figs
1½ cups dried apricots
¾ cup dried apples
1 cup pecans or walnuts
1 cup superfine sugar
6 oz white chocolate chopped
2 tablespoons butter

Place fruit in a medium bowl and cover with boiling water for 5 seconds; drain. Let stand 4 hours in covered bowl to soften fruit.

In a blender or food processor fitted with a steel blade, process fruit until texture is smooth. Add nuts and sugar and process until mixture is smooth. Spread fruit mixture evenly on waxed paper to a 8″ x 12″ square. Smooth by using a knife dipped in hot water. Cover top with additional waxed paper. Leave fruit in a cool place for 3 days to firm and dry slightly.

Melt chocolate and butter in a bowl or top of a double boiler set over a pan of simmering water. Stir until smooth. Remove waxed paper from top of fruit and spread ½ of chocolate over fruit in a thin layer. Stretch and place plastic wrap over chocolate while warm to produce a smooth finish. Let stand 3 minutes. Turn over carefully and remove waxed paper. Spread with remaining chocolate and press with plastic wrap. Refrigerate to set. When set, peel off plastic wrap. Cut into 60 small squares. Store in refrigerator up to 3 weeks.

Makes 60 pieces.

Chocolate-Coated Orange Strips

2 thick-skinned medium oranges, halved
1¼ cups sugar
1 cup water
4 oz semisweet chocolate, chopped

Squeeze juice from orange halves. Discard pieces of orange and membranes, but do not remove pith. Cut each orange skin into 10 strips, ½ inch thick. Place peel in a medium saucepan, cover with cold water and bring to boil. Repeat procedure 4 times, cooking the last time until peel is translucent. Drain well.

Combine sugar and water in a medium saucepan and cook over low heat until sugar has dissolved. Increase heat to medium–high. Continue cooking for 1 minute. Add orange strips and cook until syrup is reduced, stirring occasionally. Reduce heat if liquid begins to cook away. Place in a single layer and dry orange strips on a wire rack set over a baking sheet for 24 hours.

Melt chocolate in a bowl or top of a double boiler set over a pan of simmering water. Dip half of each orange strip in chocolate. Cool on waxed paper. Let set at room temperature. Store in a covered container in refrigerator up to 2 weeks.

Makes 80 pieces.

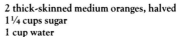

Twice Dipped Strawberries

20 medium sized to large strawberries
2 oz semisweet chocolate, chopped
2 oz white chocolate, chopped

Melt semisweet chocolate in a bowl or top of a double boiler set over a pan of simmering water. Stir until smooth.

Insert a toothpick into green hull and dip end of strawberry into chocolate. Place on a wire rack with the hull upwards to set.

Melt white chocolate in a bowl or top of a double boiler set over a pan of simmering water. Stir until smooth. Holding green hull, dip semisweet chocolate end of strawberry in white chocolate, leaving some of semisweet chocolate showing. Place on a wire rack with hull upwards to set. Chill several hours.

Makes 20 dipped strawberries.

Ginger & Date Pyramids

⅓ cup (2 oz) glacé ginger, finely chopped
½ cup (2½ oz) pitted dates, finely chopped
2 teaspoons brandy
3 oz semisweet chocolate, chopped

TO DECORATE: shredded coconut

Mix ginger, dates and brandy in a small bowl and let stand 1 hour.

Form mixture into tiny pyramids and place on waxed paper. Chill for 1 hour or until firm.

Melt chocolate in a bowl or top of a double boiler set over a pan of simmering water. Stir until smooth. Spoon chocolate over top of each pyramid. To decorate, dust top lightly with coconut. Cool until firm. Store in an airtight container with paper between layers up to 3 weeks.

Makes 12 pyramids.

Apricots with Hazelnut Filling

9 to 12 medium dried apricots, halved
½ cup hazelnuts
½ cup powdered sugar
2 teaspoons orange-flavored liqueur
1 egg white

TO COAT: 3 oz semisweet chocolate, chopped

Preheat oven to 350F (180C). In a small bowl, cover apricots with boiling water. Let stand 3 minutes. Drain and spread on paper towels to dry 1 hour. Roast hazelnuts on a baking sheet in preheated oven 10 minutes or until golden brown and skin has blistered. Wrap in a towel; let stand 5 minutes. Rub towel to remove skins. Grind nuts finely. To make filling, mix nuts with sugar, orange liqueur and sufficient egg white to form a moist paste.

Roll filling into small ovals the length of an apricot. Place filling on each apricot. Fold apricot over to enclose filling. Press apricot to make a neat shape, showing some filling. Chill 1 hour.

Melt chocolate in a bowl or top of a double boiler set over a pan of simmering water. Stir until smooth. Dip one or both ends of apricots in chocolate. Place on waxed paper until set. Refrigerate in a covered container with waxed paper between layers up to 10 days.

Makes 18 to 24 apricots.

Cherry Nut Chocolates

3 ½ oz semisweet chocolate
¼ cup macadamia nuts or blanched almonds, coarsely chopped
8 glacé cherries, quartered

Grate or chop chocolate.

Toast nuts in a dry frying pan until golden brown. Stir occasionally. Cool. Melt chocolate in a bowl or top of a double boiler set over a pan of simmering water. Stir until smooth. Drop by teaspoonfuls on waxed paper and flatten to form thick small buttons. Let partly set.

Sprinkle nuts on outside rim of chocolate. Press cherry piece in center. Let set; peel from waxed paper. Refrigerate in a covered container with waxed paper between layers up to 3 weeks.

Makes 30 chocolates.

Walnut Coffee Creams

FILLING: ¼ cup (2 fl oz) whipping cream
2 teaspoons light corn syrup
1½ teaspoons instant coffee powder
½ cup powdered sugar

3 oz semisweet chocolate, chopped
40 walnut halves or large walnut pieces

In a small saucepan, cook cream and corn syrup over low heat until corn syrup dissolves. Remove from heat; add coffee. Mix thoroughly; cool. Stir in sugar; mixture should form soft peaks. If not, add some additional sugar. Chill covered 2 hours.

Melt chocolate in a bowl or top of a double boiler set over a pan of simmering water. Stir until smooth. Drop by teaspoonfuls on waxed paper and flatten to form small chocolate buttons. Let set.

Spoon filling into a small pastry bag fitted with a fluted nozzle. Pipe a rosette around edge of each chocolate button. Leave indentation in center. Place a walnut piece in cavity. Chill 30 minutes or until firm. Remove paper. Refrigerate in a covered container with waxed paper between layers up to 2 weeks.

Makes 40 creams.

Chocolate Toffee Pecans

1¾ cups sugar
½ cup (4 fl oz) water
30 pecan or walnut halves
2 oz semisweet chocolate, chopped

Grease a baking sheet. In a small saucepan, cook sugar and water over low heat until sugar dissolves. Shake pan; do not stir. Remove sugar crystals from sides of pan with a pastry brush dipped in warm water. Adjust heat to medium; cook until a light golden brown. Transfer mixture immediately to a frying pan with small amount of water. Warm over low heat, so that toffee does not set too quickly.

Drop 6 nuts in pan. Swirl pan gently to coat. Remove each one with a small teaspoon. Do not stir or shake toffee. Place nuts on prepared baking sheet. Let set. Repeat with remaining nuts.

Melt chocolate in a bowl or top of a double boiler set over a pan of simmering water. Stir until smooth. Scoop a little chocolate in a spoon. Dip one end of each toffee-coated nut. Let set on waxed paper. Refrigerate in an airtight container with waxed paper between layers up to 5 weeks.

Makes 30 pieces.

Chocolate-Coated Macadamias

18 whole macadamia nuts, whole almonds or walnut
halves
2 oz semisweet chocolate, chopped
2 oz white chocolate, chopped

Insert a toothpick in each nut.

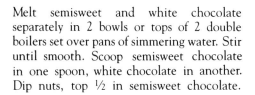

Melt semisweet and white chocolate
separately in 2 bowls or tops of 2 double
boilers set over pans of simmering water. Stir
until smooth. Scoop semisweet chocolate
in one spoon, white chocolate in another.
Dip nuts, top ½ in semisweet chocolate.

Dip bottom ½ of each nut in white
chocolate. Stick toothpicks into an orange
or grapefruit to set evenly. Refrigerate in a
covered container up to 1 week.

Makes 18 pieces.

Chocolate Almond Toffee

1¾ cups sugar
½ cup water
1 teaspoon vanilla extract
½ cup slivered almonds
2 oz semisweet chocolate, chopped

Lightly grease a 11″ x 7″ pan. Combine sugar and water in a saucepan over low heat. Swirl pan to dissolve sugar. When sugar is dissolved, boil until mixture is a pale golden color. Remove from heat and add vanilla. Swirl pan to combine and pour toffee into prepared pan.

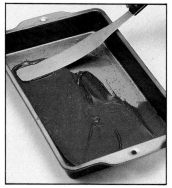

Place almonds on a baking sheet and toast 10 minutes at 350F (180C), stir occasionally, until almonds are a golden color. Cool. Melt chocolate in a bowl or top of a double boiler set over a pan of simmering water. Stir until smooth. When toffee is firmly set, spread chocolate evenly over toffee using back of a spoon or a small knife.

Sprinkle with almonds and press almonds into chocolate. Let set until firm. Run a sharp knife around the edges. Invert on waxed paper and break toffee into small pieces. Store in an airtight container in the refrigerator up to 1 month.

Makes about 50 pieces.

Chocolate Hazelnut Buttons

FILLING: ½ cup hazelnuts
2 oz semisweet chocolate, chopped
¼ cup unsalted butter, diced
1 tablespoon brandy

BUTTONS: 3 oz white chocolate, chopped

TO DECORATE: slices of hazelnut
grated white chocolate

Place hazelnuts on a baking sheet and toast at 350F (180C) until skins are slightly blistered. Wrap hazelnuts in a towel for 3 minutes. Remove skins by rubbing with towel. Chop nuts finely. To make filling, place semisweet chocolate, butter and brandy in a bowl or top of a double boiler set over a pan of simmering water. Stir until smooth. Remove from heat, stir in nuts and cool. Refrigerate filling 1 hour or until firm enough to handle.

Melt white chocolate in a bowl or top of a double boiler. Set over simmering water. Stir until smooth. Form buttons by dropping 1 teaspoon of white chocolate onto waxed paper. Smooth out each button to form a flat round.

Form ½ teaspoon of filling into a tiny ball and flatten ball so it is same size as white chocolate button. While white chocolate is still soft, top button with hazelnut filling. Lightly press together. Decorate each button with a slice of hazelnut or grated white chocolate. Refrigerate for 2 hours or until set. To store, layer in a jar leaving each one attached to small piece of waxed paper up to 3 weeks.

Makes 24 buttons.

Chocolate Drambuie Strips

¼ cup (2 fl oz) whipping cream
5 oz milk chocolate, chopped
2 tablespoons Drambuie

TO FINISH: powdered sugar, sifted

Line bottom of baking sheet with waxed paper. Heat cream in a small saucepan until bubbling around edges. Remove from heat and add chocolate. Let stand, covered, until chocolate melts. Add Drambuie and mix well. Refrigerate until firm enough to hold soft peaks.

Using a fluted nozzle in a pastry bag, pipe strips onto waxed paper. Place immediately in freezer to set.

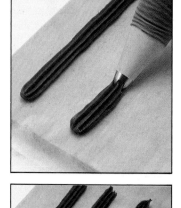

Cut chocolate into strips. Store in freezer with paper between layers for up to 3 months. Remove from the freezer just before serving, as they become creamy within 20 minutes at room temperature. Dust with powdered sugar.

Makes 40 pieces.

Coffee Creams

CASES: 4 oz white chocolate, chopped

COFFEE CREAM FILLING: 4 tablespoons whipping cream
2 oz white chocolate, chopped
2 teaspoons coffee liqueur
2 teaspoons instant coffee powder, dissolved in
   1 teaspoon water

TO DECORATE: 24 slices brazil nuts

Line bottom of baking sheet with waxed paper. To make cases, melt chocolate in a bowl or top of a double boiler set over a pan of simmering water. Brush a thin layer of chocolate on bottom and sides of small foil cases. Turn cases upside down on baking sheet. Refrigerate to set. Remove and brush a second layer of chocolate on top of first layer. Turn cases upside down on baking sheet. Refrigerate to set.

To make filling, heat cream in a small saucepan until boiling. Add chocolate, and remove from heat. Let stand, covered, until chocolate melts. Mix in coffee liqueur and coffee; stir until smooth.

Fill cases with filling. Decorate with a slice of brazil nut. Chill until set. Peel off foil cases before serving. To store, refrigerate in a covered container up to 1 week.

Makes 24 creams.

Mocha Creams

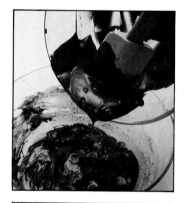

6 oz semisweet chocolate, chopped
1/4 cup butter
1 tablespoon instant coffee powder granules
1 egg yolk
2 teaspoons rum
2 oz white chocolate, chopped

Line bottom of baking sheet with waxed paper. Melt semisweet chocolate in a bowl or top of a double boiler set over a pan of simmering water; cool. In a medium bowl, cream butter until soft; add instant coffee. Stir in cooled chocolate, egg yolk, and rum. Chill slightly until mixture is of piping consistency.

Using a fluted nozzle in a pastry bag, pipe small rounds with peaks on top on baking sheet. Chill until set.

Melt white chocolate in a bowl or top of a double boiler set over a pan of simmering water. Hold mocha creams by base. Dip peaked tops into white chocolate to coat. Place on baking sheet. Refrigerate to chill. When set, store in a covered container in refrigerator up to 2 weeks.

Makes 40 creams.

Chocolate Cups

4oz semisweet or milk chocolate, chopped
24 foil petits four cases

Place a sheet of waxed paper on a baking sheet. Melt chocolate in a bowl or top of a double boiler set over a pan of simmering water. Stir until smooth; cool slightly. Spoon 1 teaspoon melted chocolate into each foil case. Spread chocolate over bottom and up sides of cases with back of spoon covering insides completely. Place upside-down on prepared baking sheet. Refrigerate 20 minutes or until chocolate is completely set.

Using a pastry brush, recoat insides of cases with remaining melted chocolate. Place on baking sheet. Refrigerate until set.

Refrigerate cups in a sealed container. To serve, fill cups, see pages 26, 27, 28, and peel off foil.

Makes 24 cups.

Lemon-Filled Chocolate Cups

18 chocolate cups, page 25

1 teaspoon unflavored gelatin
1 tablespoon cold water
3 tablespoons yogurt
¼ teaspoon grated lemon peel
1 teaspoon lemon juice
1 teaspoon brandy
2 tablespoons powdered sugar
1 tablespoon whipping cream

TO DECORATE: 1 oz semisweet or milk chocolate, chopped

Dissolve gelatin in water in a small mixing bowl or jug placed in pan of hot water.

Mix yogurt with lemon peel, lemon juice, brandy, sugar and cream. Add yogurt mixture by spoonfuls to gelatine and blend.

Fill chocolate cups quickly before gelatin sets. Refrigerate filled cups for 2 days or until set. To decorate, melt chocolate in small saucepan over low heat. Spoon chocolate into a pastry bag fitted with a small plain writing tip. Pipe chocolate in a small spiral on top of filling. Refrigerate until set. Store up to 2 days. To serve, peel off foil.

Makes 18 cups.

Cherry Liqueur-Filled Cups

12 chocolate cups, page 25

FILLING: 12 pitted sour cherries
2 tablespoons kirsch, brandy or cognac
1 tablespoon whipping cream
1 teaspoon light corn syrup
1 oz white chocolate, chopped

Combine cherries and kirsch, brandy or cognac in a small bowl. Cover and refrigerate for 3 days. Stir occasionally. Drain cherries; reserve the kirsch. Place a cherry in a foil-covered chocolate cup.

In a small saucepan, cook cream and corn syrup until cream is bubbling. Add chocolate; remove from heat. Cover and let stand until chocolate melts. Stir until smooth. Add reserved kirsch from cherries.

Cover cherry in chocolate cup with chocolate mixture. Refrigerate up to 3 weeks. To serve peel off foil.

Makes 12 cups.

Fruit-Filled Chocolate Cups

12 chocolate cups, page 25

FILLING: ¼ cup (1½ oz) mixed glacé fruit, made up of equal parts glacé cherries, apricots, pineapple and ginger, finely chopped
1 tablespoon brandy
1 rounded tablespoon lightly-whipped cream

TO DECORATE: 12 thin slices glacé cherry

Combine fruit and brandy in a small bowl. Cover and refrigerate for 24 hours.

Fold cream through fruit mixture. Fill chocolate cups and smooth top.

Decorate with a thin slice of cherry. Refrigerate until firm. To serve, peel off foil.

Makes 12 cups.

Praline

⅓ cup almond slivers or hazelnuts
½ cup sugar
¼ cup water

Place nuts on a baking sheet and toast at
350F (180C) for 10 minutes or until golden
brown. Stir occasionally to color evenly. If
using hazelnuts, chop finely. Lightly oil
another baking sheet. In a medium
saucepan, heat sugar and water over low
heat until sugar dissolves, shaking pan
occasionally. Increase heat and cook until
golden and sugary. Stir in nuts.

Cook 2–3 minutes, stirring well.

Pour onto prepared sheet; cool. When
brittle, finely crush with a meat mallet or
process in a blender or processor. Store in an
airtight container in refrigerator 3 weeks.
Use in truffles, pages 30 and 31, and Praline
and Orange Puffs, page 105.

Makes ¾ cup crushed praline.

Almond Praline Truffles

⅓ cup butter, cubed
½ cup (4 fl oz) whipping cream
10 oz milk chocolate, chopped
2 egg yolks
¾ cup crushed almond praline, page 29
unsweetened cocoa powder

In a small saucepan, combine butter with cream. Cook on low heat until butter melts and cream bubbles around edges.

Remove from heat; add chocolate. Cover and let stand until chocolate melts. Stir until smooth. Add egg yolks, one at a time. Stir over a low heat until glossy. Mixture should be tepid. Remove from heat; cool. Fold in crushed praline. Refrigerate until firm.

Form into 60 balls. Roll in cocoa and coat completely. Chill until firm. Refrigerate in an airtight container up to 10 days. To serve, place in small paper or foil cases.

Makes 60 truffles.

Hazelnut Praline Truffles

¼ cup butter, cubed
8 oz semisweet chocolate, chopped
½ cup (4 fl oz) whipping cream
1 tablespoon dark rum
¾ cup hazelnut praline, page 29

TO COAT: 1½ oz semisweet chocolate, chopped
1½ oz milk chocolate, chopped

Melt butter in a small saucepan. Remove from heat and add chocolate. Cover and let stand 3 minutes. Stir until smooth. Add cream a few spoonfuls at a time, stirring well until chocolate is smooth.

Cool mixture. Add rum. Mix in crushed hazelnut praline and stir well. Refrigerate until firm. Form into 60 small balls. Refrigerate to firm.

To coat the truffles, melt semisweet chocolate in a bowl or top of a double boiler set over a pan of simmering water. Stir until smooth. Repeat procedure for milk chocolate. Dip tops of 30 truffles into semisweet chocolate. Dip the tops of remaining 30 into milk chocolate. Place on waxed paper, chocolate side uppermost. Let set at room temperature. Refrigerate in a covered container with waxed paper between layers up to 10 days.

Makes about 60 truffles.

White Truffles

¼ cup slivered almonds
2 tablespoons finely chopped mixed glacé fruit
3 tablespoons whipping cream
3½ oz white chocolate, chopped
1 tablespoon kirsch or brandy

TO COAT: ½ cup (1½ oz) shredded coconut

Toast almonds in a dry frying pan until golden, stirring occasionally. Chop finely. In a small bowl mix almonds with glacé fruits.

Bring cream to a boil in a small saucepan. Add chocolate to cream. Cover and let stand until chocolate softens. Stir until smooth. Mix in kirsch or brandy, nuts and fruit. Refrigerate in a bowl until firm.

Toast coconut in a dry frying pan. Stir until golden; cool. Form truffle mixture into 24 balls. Roll balls in coconut. Store in refrigerator up to 10 days. To serve, place in small paper or foil cases.

Makes 24 truffles.

Orange Truffles

¼ cup butter, chopped
⅓ cup (2½ fl oz) whipping cream
7 oz semisweet chocolate, chopped
1 egg yolk
1 teaspoon grated orange peel
2 tablespoons finely chopped mixed citrus peel
2 tablespoons Grand Marnier
unsweetened cocoa powder

In a small saucepan, combine butter and cream. Cook on low heat until butter melts and cream bubbles around edge. Remove from heat; add chocolate. Cover and let stand until chocolate melts. Stir until smooth.

Stir in egg yolk. Mix in orange peel, citrus peel, and Grand Marnier. Chill until firm.

Form into 40 balls. Roll in cocoa. Refrigerate in an airtight container up to 2 weeks. To serve, place in small paper or foil cases.

Makes 40 truffles.

Two-Toned Truffles

WHITE CENTER: 2 teaspoons light corn syrup
$\frac{1}{4}$ cup (2 fl oz) whipping cream
5 oz white chocolate, chopped

CHOCOLATE COATING: $\frac{1}{4}$ cup butter, chopped
$6\frac{1}{2}$ oz semisweet chocolate, chopped
3 tablespoons whipping cream
2 tablespoons Grand Marnier
unsweetened cocoa powder

To make white center, combine corn syrup and cream in a small saucepan. Bring to a boil. Remove from heat and add white chocolate. Leave stand few minutes until white chocolate melts and, if necessary, return to low heat. Pour mixture into a medium bowl lined with foil. Chill until firm. Form mixture into 6 balls. Freeze until firm.

To make chocolate coating, melt butter in a small saucepan on low heat. Add semisweet chocolate; remove from heat. Stir until smooth. Add cream and Grand Marnier. Chill until slightly firm. To assemble truffles, divide semisweet chocolate mixture into 6 balls. Flatten each ball. Wrap around white chocolate ball. Roll between hands to form an even surface.

Roll balls in cocoa. Freeze until firm. Wrap each ball in plastic wrap and then in foil. Store in freezer up to 8 weeks. To serve, cut each frozen ball in $\frac{1}{2}$, using a knife dipped in boiling water. Divide each $\frac{1}{2}$ into 3 wedges. Place in small paper cases, white side up.

Makes 36 truffles.

Ginger Truffles

¼ cup butter, cubed
⅓ cup (2½ fl oz) whipping cream
½ teaspoon fresh ginger
6½ oz milk chocolate, chopped
¼ cup (1½ oz) finely chopped glacé ginger
1 egg yolk
1 tablespoon Drambuie
unsweetened cocoa powder

Grate fresh ginger. In a small saucepan, combine butter with cream and fresh ginger. Cook on low heat until butter melts and cream bubbles around edge.

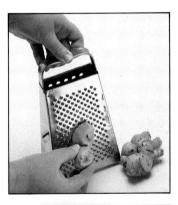

Remove from heat. Add chocolate. Cover and let stand until chocolate melts. Stir until smooth. Mix in glacé ginger and egg yolk. Add Drambuie. Chill 8 hours or until firm.

Form into 40 small balls. Roll in cocoa. Refrigerate up to 3 weeks. To serve, place in small paper or foil cases.

Makes 40 truffles.

Cake Truffles

1 ½ cups sponge or butter cake crumbs
grated peel ½ orange
grated peel ½ lemon
2 teaspoons powdered sugar
2 teaspoons apricot jam, sieved smooth
2 tablespoons finely chopped glacé cherries
½ teaspoon lemon juice
unsweetened cocoa powder

Place cake crumbs in a medium bowl. Add orange and lemon peel, sugar, jam, cherries and lemon juice. Mix well. If not moist enough to stick together, add a little extra lemon juice.

Form into 20 small balls. Sift cocoa on to waxed paper.

Roll balls in cocoa until lightly coated. Shake gently to rid excess cocoa. Refrigerate in a covered container up to 5 days. To serve place in small paper or foil cases.

Makes 20 truffles.

Almond & Prune Truffles

8 pitted prunes, chopped
2 tablespoons cognac
2 tablespoons blanched almonds, finely chopped
½ cup (4 fl oz) whipping cream
6 oz semisweet chocolate, chopped
2 tablespoons butter, melted
unsweetened cocoa powder

Cover prunes with cognac in a small bowl. Let stand 2 hours. Toast almonds in a dry frying pan until light brown. Stir occasionally.

Heat cream in a small saucepan until bubbling around edge. Add chocolate. Remove from heat. Cover and let stand 5 minutes. Stir until smooth. Stir in butter. Drain liquid from prunes. Stir liquid into chocolate mixture. Stir in almonds and prune pieces. Chill until slighty firm.

Form into 40 balls. Roll in cocoa. Refrigerate with waxed paper between layers up to 2 weeks. To serve, place in small paper or foil cases.

Makes 40 truffles.

Rum Balls

RUM BALLS: ³/₄ cup génoise crumbs, page 55
¹/₄ cup powdered sugar
¹/₄ cup ground almonds
2 teaspoons dark rum
1 teaspoon lemon juice
1¹/₂ oz semisweet chocolate, chopped
2 tablespoons whipping cream

ICING: ¹/₃ cup powdered sugar
2 tablespoons butter, chopped
1 oz semisweet chocolate, grated
2 teaspoons dark rum
warm water

TO DECORATE: chocolate sprinkles

In a medium bowl, combine cake crumbs, sugar, almonds, rum and lemon juice. Melt chocolate in a bowl or top of a double boiler set over a pan of simmering water. Add to rum mixture with sufficient cream for mixture to hold together when pressed between fingers. Form teaspoonfuls of mixture into 18 small balls. Refrigerate on a baking sheet 4 hours or until firm.

To make icing, combine sugar, butter, chocolate and rum in a small saucepan. When chocolate and butter softens, add a tablespoon of water. Warm again and add sufficient water to liquify.

To coat rum balls, insert a poultry skewer in center of a rum ball. Tilt pan of icing and dip each ball. Let excess drip. To decorate, roll in chocolate sprinkles to coat completely. Refrigerate in a covered container with waxed paper between layers up to 10 days.

Makes 18 rum balls.

Christmas Truffles

¾ cup (3 oz) vanilla cookies, crushed
2 tablespoons finely chopped glacé cherries
2 tablespoons finely chopped hazelnuts
2 tablespoons ground almonds
2 tablespoons finely chopped mixed citrus peel
2 tablespoons chopped raisins
1 tablespoon brandy or rum
2 drops almond extract
¼ cup (2 oz) butter, cubed
6 oz semisweet chocolate, chopped
2 tablespoons whipping cream

TO COAT: ¾ cup (3 oz) finely chopped hazelnuts

In a medium bowl, mix cookies, cherries, hazelnuts, almonds, peel, raisins, brandy or rum and almond extract.

Melt butter in a small saucepan until bubbling. Add chocolate; remove from heat. Cover and let stand. Stir occasionally, until chocolate melts. Add cream; stir into cookie mixture. Refrigerate until firm.

Form into 40 small balls. To coat, roll balls in nuts. Refrigerate in a covered container with waxed paper between layers up to 2 weeks. To serve, place in small paper or foil cases.

Makes 40 truffles.

Marzipan

2 cups ground almonds
1¾ cup powdered sugar, sifted
2 teaspoons lemon juice
2 teaspoons sherry or brandy
2 drops almond extract, if desired
2 small egg whites
powdered sugar

Combine almonds and sugar in a medium bowl. Add lemon juice, sherry or brandy, and almond extract, if desired.

Gradually mix in enough egg white to ensure that paste is sticky, but not wet.

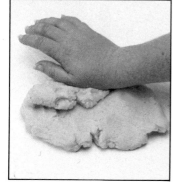

Knead paste until smooth on a pastry board dusted with powdered sugar. Wrap in plastic wrap. Store in refrigerator up to 4 weeks. To use, see pages 41, 42, 43, 44, 47, 49, 56, 118.

Makes 1 pound.

Marzipan Cherry Delights

3½ oz marzipan, page 40
pink food coloring
1 teaspoon kirsch
3 oz semisweet chocolate, chopped
6 peeled pistachio nuts

Line a plate with waxed paper. Knead marzipan with food coloring to shade of pale pink. Add sufficient kirsch so marzipan is slightly sticky but able to hold a shape. Form into 18 small balls. Place on waxed paper and refrigerate until firm.

Melt chocolate in a bowl or top of a double boiler set over a pan of simmering water. Stir until smooth. Insert a toothpick in top of each marzipan ball. Dip ½ of ball into chocolate. Place balls on waxed paper and refrigerate to dry and firm.

Cut pistachio nuts in 3 pieces lengthwise. Remove toothpicks and insert pistachio nuts in cavity left by toothpick. Store in a covered container in refrigerator up to 10 days.

Makes 18 balls.

Chocolate Marzipan Delights

1 oz semisweet chocolate
4 oz homemade marzipan, page 40
1 egg white
peppermint extract
3 oz white chocolate, chopped
24 angelica strips
grate or chop semisweet chocolate

Grate or chop semisweet chocolate.

Melt semisweet chocolate in a bowl or top of a double boiler set over a pan of simmering water. Gradually add chocolate to marzipan and knead well. If marzipan becomes dry, add 1 to 2 teaspoons of egg white. Flavor with a few drops of peppermint extract. Form into 24 small balls. Chill for 1 hour to firm.

Melt white chocolate in a bowl or top of a double boiler set over a pan of simmering water. Insert a toothpick in top of each marzipan ball and dip base of ball in chocolate. Place on waxed paper to set. Remove toothpick and insert a strip of angelica in cavity left by toothpick. Store in refrigerator in one layer so balls retain stalks. These will keep for about 10 days.

Makes 24 balls.

Marzipan Cherry Log

4 oz marzipan, page 40
2 tablespoons powdered sugar
1/3 cup (1 oz) shredded coconut
1 egg white
1/4 cup pistachio nuts, shelled
green food coloring
6-8 glacé cherries

TO DECORATE: 1/2 cup (1 1/2 oz) shredded coconut

Mix marzipan, powdered sugar, 1/3 cup coconut and egg white in a medium mixing bowl. Mixture should be moist, but not sticky. Knead well; divide into 2 sections. Wrap each section in plastic wrap; chill for 2 hours. Place nuts in a small bowl. Cover with boiling water. Let stand until water is tepid to remove brown skins. Peel and finely chop nuts. Mix nuts and 2 drops green food coloring with 1 marzipan section.

On a powdered sugared surface or between 2 sheets of plastic wrap, roll thinly to 8" × 4". Roll second section in same way, trim edges and sides evenly. Top green section with plain section. Cut cherries in 1/2 and place flat side down in center of rectangle. Roll 2 sections to enclose cherries.

Toast 1/2 cup coconut in a dry frying pan, stirring until light golden brown. Roll log in coconut to completely coat outside. If marzipan is dry, use a pastry brush to moisten with a little water, so coconut will stick. Refrigerate log wrapped in foil. Slice just before serving.

Makes 30 slices.

— Marzipan Fruits and Vegetables —

marzipan, page 40
superfine sugar
food coloring

Mold fruits or vegetables. Dry for 1 day. Paint with food coloring. Cover and refrigerate up to 10 days.

Apple: Form a small ball. Curve sides gently. Make base slightly pointed. Press indentations into sides and top where stalk is attached. Paint red with tinges of green and brown. Place a small clove or a small piece of a strawberry or cherry stalk on top.

Banana: Form a long piece of marzipan, thinner at ends than at center. Bend slightly to curve. Paint yellow with streaks of brown or green. Use a piece of cherry stalk or clove to make end.

Lemon: Form a ball. Make rounded points at both ends. Gently pinch one point to make an indentation. Paint yellow and tint points light green. Roll on a nutmeg grater to make indents.

Mushroom: Form 2 balls of marzipan. Flatten in 2 rounds. One round should be slightly larger. Place smaller round on top of larger round; fold over edge. Lightly cut inside to resemble markings of a mushroom cap. Form piece of marzipan into a stalk. Place stalk in center of lower round. Paint outside pale cream to light brown and inside dark brown.

Pear: Form a small ball. Stretch one end slightly to form a pear shape. Paint pale green or yellow. Paint diluted red on rounded section to give a ripe appearance. Place a small piece of strawberry or cherry stalk on tapered end.

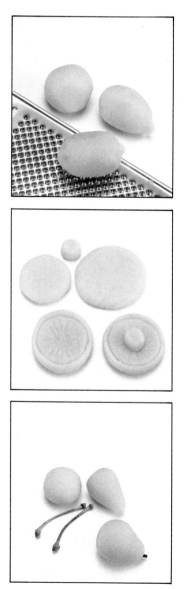

Marzipan Fruits Continued

Strawberry: Form a small ball of marzipan. Pinch slightly to make base longer. Point should be slightly rounded and top flattened. Paint with red coloring. While coloring is wet, drop strawberry into superfine sugar. Add a small green leaf of molded or cut green marzipan.

Watermelon Slices: Form a ball. Flatten into a circle. Cut in ½. Let dry. Paint outside dark green. Leave a strip of natural colored marzipan inside. Paint flat sides and straight edges pink. When dry, paint dark brown seeds.

Orange: Make a small ball. Roll over a grater to make imprints. When dry, paint orange. Attach a tiny piece of stalk, if desired.

Chocolate Marzipan Log

4 oz marzipan, crumbled, page 40
¼ cup (1½ oz) powdered sugar
1 egg white
¾ cup (2¼ oz) shredded coconut
angelica strips or glacé apricots, halved
1½ oz semisweet chocolate, chopped

In a medium bowl, mix marzipan and sugar. Knead small amounts of egg white into marzipan mixture. Add additional egg white until a sticky paste forms. Add coconut and knead for 1 minute. If too sticky, knead on a powdered sugar surface. Chill mixture 30 minutes.

Form a long roll 12″ x 6″ on plastic wrap. Place angelica strips or glacé apricots along one side. Roll marzipan over to enclose fruit. Wrap well; chill 12 hours.

Melt chocolate in a bowl or top of a double boiler set over a pan of simmering water. Stir until smooth. Unwrap almond roll and spread one side with chocolate. When set, turn log over and spread chocolate on other side. When set, wrap and chill. Refrigerate whole up to 3 weeks. To serve, cut into slices as needed.

Makes 24 slices

Glazed Apricot Pecans

40 pecan or walnut halves

APRICOT PURÉE:
¼ (2 oz) cup + 2 tablespoons dried apricots
2 tablespoons powdered sugar
¼ cup (1 oz) ground almonds
1 teaspoon brandy

TOFFEE: 1 cup sugar
⅓ cup (2½ fl oz) water

In a small saucepan, cook apricots covered with water until soft. Drain; and purée apricots.

In a medium, bowl, combine apricots, powdered sugar almonds and brandy. Chill 2 hours before using. Refrigerate up to 2 days. Place a teaspoon of apricot mixture on a nut; top with another nut. Press together gently. Remove excess apricot mixture.

Grease a wire rack and baking sheet. Place wire rack over baking sheet. In a small saucepan, cook sugar and water over low heat. Swirl mixture occasionally until sugar dissolves. Adjust heat to medium. Cook until mixture is a light golden brown. Remove from heat. Quickly drop nuts, one-by-one, into toffee. Using a small spoon, remove immediately; cool on wire rack. Refrigerate in a covered container up to 12 hours.

Makes 20 pieces

French Prunes

16 dessert prunes
2 oz marzipan, page 40
green food coloring

TOFFEE COATING: 1¼ cups sugar
⅓ cup (2½ fl oz) water

In a small bowl, cover prunes with boiling water. Let stand 15 minutes. Drain and spread on paper towels. Cut a slit in one side of each prune; remove pit.

Knead marzipan, add 1 to 2 drops green food coloring. Form marzipan into 16 balls. Roll balls to an oval. Insert shaped marzipan into prune cavity left by pit. Mold prune to leave green section showing. Let dry for 3 hours.

To make toffee, warm sugar and water in a small saucepan over low heat until sugar has dissolved. Adjust heat to medium; cook until mixture turns light golden brown. Shake pan occasionally. Brush sugar granules on side of pan away with a pastry brush dipped in cold water. Remove from heat. Pierce each prune through side with a toothpick. Place prunes on a wire rack set over a jelly-roll pan. Tilt saucepan of toffee. Quickly dip each prune holding by toothpick or dipping tool to coat with toffee. Let stand on wire rack until set. Refrigerate in a single layer up to 12 hours.

Makes 16 prunes.

Caramel-Glazed Fruit

12 medium-sized strawberries
or 12 mandarin segments
or 18 cherries
or 10 bunches of grapes, 2 grapes to 1 bunch

CARAMEL: 1½ cups sugar
⅓ cup (2½ fl oz) water
pinch of cream of tartar

If using grapes or cherries, wash and let drain 2 hours on paper towels. If using strawberries, clean with a pastry brush. Leave stalks on fruit. If using mandarins, peel fruit and separate segments. Remove membrane. Dry mandarin segments on a wire rack 3-4 hours. Push a wooden pick into mandarin segments.

Lightly grease a baking sheet to make caramel, in a small saucepan, warm sugar and water over low heat until sugar has dissolved. Shake pan occasionally. When sugar has dissolved, add cream of tartar. Adjust heat to high; cook until caramel becomes light gold. Brush away sugar crystals on side of pan away with a pastry brush dipped in cold water. Do not stir syrup.

Immediately dip fruits. Let excess caramel drip over saucepan. Place on prepared baking sheet. Let stand until set. Place in paper cases and serve within 4 hours.

Makes 10-18 pieces.

Apricot & Ginger Balls

3 tablespoons hazelnuts
10 dried apricot halves
1 tablespoon finely chopped glacé ginger
2 teaspoons powdered sugar

TO COVER: ½ cup ground almonds
¼ cup powdered sugar
1 teaspoon lemon juice
egg white

TOPPING: ½ cup almonds, finely chopped

Preheat oven to 350F (180C). Roast hazelnuts in preheated oven on baking sheet 10 minutes or until golden brown and skins have slightly blistered. Wrap in a towel; let stand 2 minutes. Rub them in the towel to remove skins. Chop nuts finely. In a small saucepan, cook apricots covered with water, until softened. Drain; dry on paper towels. Chop apricots.

In a small bowl mix hazelnuts, apricots, ginger and sugar. Refrigerate 1 hour or until firm. Form mixture into 18 small balls. Refrigerate on a plate. To make covering, in a small bowl, mix ground almonds, sugar and lemon juice. Add ½ to 1 teaspoon egg white to form a sticky but firm paste. Chill 2 hours.

Form 18 small balls from covering mixture. Flatten; place an apricot ginger ball in center. Fold to partly enclose. Leave top of apricot ball showing. Dip apricot top in chopped almonds to coat thickly. Refrigerate in a covered container with waxed paper between layers up to 10 days.

Makes 18 balls.

Fruit Pyramids

¼ cup + 2 tablespoons dried figs, chopped
¼ cup + 2 tablespoons pitted dates, finely chopped
3 tablespoons glacé cherries, finely chopped
¼ cup + 2 tablespoons dried apricots, finely chopped
⅓ cup (2 oz) pine nuts, finely chopped
2 teaspoons lemon juice
⅓ cup powdered sugar
TO COAT: shredded coconut

In a small bowl, mix figs, dates and cherries. Cover apricots with boiling water in a small bowl. Let stand 2 minutes. Drain well; add to other fruit.

Mix pine nuts, lemon juice and sugar with fruit. Mixture should bind together when pressed between fingers. If too firm, moisten with lemon juice.

Toast coconut in a dry skillet. Stir frequently until a pale golden brown. Form fruit mixture into 36 small balls. Roll in coconut. Pinch tops to form pyramids. Chill 2 hours on a plate. Refrigerate in a covered container in a single layer or with foil between layers up to 3 weeks.

Makes 36 pieces.

Candied Grapefruit Peel

2 large thick skinned grapefruit
1 ½ cups sugar
1 cup (8 fl oz) water
superfine sugar

Cut each grapefruit in ½; discard pulp. Cut each ½ of peel in 4 pieces. Cut peel pieces in triangular shapes or strips. Each grapefruit should yield about 40 pieces.

In a small saucepan, bring grapefruit peel, covered with cold water, to a boil over medium heat. Drain. Repeat procedure 6 times, cooking peel the last time until soft. Drain. In a small saucepan, cook sugar and water over low heat until sugar dissolves. Adjust heat to medium, bring to a boil. Add pieces of peel. Cook uncovered until sections are clear and transparent. Using a slotted spoon, remove peel to a wire rack set over a baking sheet. Separate pieces; let set 48 hours or until firm.

In a medium bowl, dust peel with sugar. Dry on a wire rack 6 hours. Refrigerate in a covered container up to 4 weeks.

Makes about 80 pieces.

Honey Nut Fruit Balls

¾ cup (3 oz) pine nuts
1 tablespoon vegetable oil
¼ cup + 2 tablespoons glacé cherries, finely chopped
¼ cup + 2 tablespoons pitted dates, finely chopped
¼ cup + 2 tablespoons mixed citrus peel, chopped
¾ cup pecans, finely chopped
½ teaspoon cinnamon
2 tablespoons honey
½ cup ground almonds
1 egg white

In a skillet, fry pine nuts with oil over medium heat. Stir until nuts are golden brown. Drain on paper towels. Chop medium fine.

In a small bowl, mix all fruits with pecans and cinnamon. In a small saucepan, warm honey over low heat. Add honey to fruits; mix well. Add ground almonds and enough egg white so mixture will hold together when pressed between fingers. Cool 15 minutes.

Form into 50 small balls. Roll balls in pine nuts to lightly coat. Chill on a plate. Refrigerate in an airtight container with waxed paper between layers up to 2 weeks. To serve, place in small paper or foil cases.

Makes 50 balls

Plain Génoise

3 eggs
½ cup superfine sugar
1 teaspoon vanilla extract
¾ cup all-purpose flour, sifted
2 tablespoons butter, melted and cooled

Preheat oven to 350F (180C). Grease and flour bottom and sides of a 14″ x 10″ baking pan. Shake out excess flour.

Combine eggs and sugar in a medium mixing bowl. Place bowl in a pan of hot water. Beat until mixture is very thick and just warm. Mixture should form a ribbon when beaters are lifted. Remove from heat and add vanilla. Continue beating until mixture is almost cool. Fold flour into egg and sugar mixture. Mix in butter.

Pour batter into prepared greased pan; level top. Bake in a preheated oven 20-25 minutes or until set on top. Cool pan on a wire rack 10 minutes. Run a knife carefully around the edge. Remove from pan. Cool completely on wire rack. Use within 36 hours or wrap and freeze up to 6 weeks. To use, see pages 38, 56, 60, 64.

Makes one 14″ x 10″ cake.

Iced Petits Fours

1/3 génoise, page 55

TOPPING: 1/2 cup apricot jam or preserve
1 tablespoon water
1/2 (3 1/2 oz) marzipan, page 40

ICING: 1 tablespoon light corn syrup
1/4 cup warm water
2 cups powdered sugar
few drops food coloring, if desired

To make topping, press jam through a fine strainer into a small saucepan; stir in water. Cook, stirring, 1-2 minutes or until mixture is smooth. Cool slightly. Brush over top of cake.

Roll out marzipan thinly between 2 sheets of waxed paper. Remove 1 sheet of waxed paper from marzipan. Invert marzipan on top of cake; peel off waxed paper.

Trim marzipan edges even with cake. Chill 30 minutes.

Using a very sharp knife, cut cake into 1-inch squares and chill to firm. Place on a wire rack set over a baking sheet.

If making round petits fours, use a pastry cutter to cut circles of cake. Brush top and sides with topping. Cut circles of marzipan with pastry cutter. Place on top of cake. To coat sides, roll on strip of marzipan.

To make icing, combine corn syrup and 2 tablespoons water in a bowl or top of a double boiler set over a pan of simmering water. Add powdered sugar and mix well. Add 1 to 2 more tablespoons of warm water. Warm until mixture is smooth. Tint with food coloring, if desired. Carefully spoon icing over marzipanned cake. Leave to set. Decorate with flowers or fruit or pipe with melted chocolate.

Makes 27 petits fours.

Chocolate Génoise

3 eggs
½ cup superfine sugar
½ teaspoon vanilla extract
½ cup all-purpose flour
¼ teaspoon ground cinnamon
¼ cup unsweetened cocoa powder
2 tablespoons butter, melted and cooled

Preheat oven to 350F (180C). Grease and flour bottom and sides of a 14″ x 10″ baking pan. Shake off excess flour. Combine eggs and sugar in a medium mixing bowl. Place bowl in a pan of hot water. Beat until mixture is very thick and just warm. Mixture should form a ribbon when beaters are lifted. Remove from heat and add vanilla. Continue beating until mixture is almost cool. Sift flour, cinnamon and cocoa together. Fold ½ of flour mixture in to egg and sugar. Repeat with remaining flour mixture.

Mix in butter. Pour batter into prepared greased pan; level top. Bake in preheated oven 30-35 minutes or until set on top. Cool pan on a wire rack 10 minutes.

Run knife carefully around edge. Remove from pan. Cool completely on a wire rack. Use within 24 hours or wrap and freeze up to 6 weeks. To use, see page 62.

Makes one 14″ x 10″ cake.

Petits Fours Siciliana

CAKE: 3 egg yolks
3 tablespoons sugar
2 tablespoons unsweetened cocoa powder
1 teaspoon vanilla extract
3 egg whites

FILLING: ¾ cup ricotta or cottage cheese
3 tablespoons powdered sugar
2 tablespoons orange liqueur
1½ tablespoons finely-chopped mixed citrus peel
3 tablespoons grated semisweet chocolate

TO COAT: unsweetened cocoa powder

Preheat oven to 350F (180C). Grease bottom and sides 11½" x 8½" baking pan. Line the bottom with waxed paper. Grease and lightly flour paper. Shake off excess flour. In a medium bowl, beat egg yolks with sugar until light. Sift in cocoa; add vanilla. In a small bowl, beat egg whites until stiff. Gently fold into egg yolks, ½ at a time.

Spread mixture evenly in prepared pan. Bake in preheated oven 10 to 12 minutes or until set. Cool in pan on wire rack 10 minutes. Invert cake on waxed paper; peel waxed paper off bottom of cake. To store cake, wrap in plastic wrap up to 24 hours.

To make filling, in a small bowl, beat or process cheese until smooth. Add sugar, orange liqueur, peel and chocolate. Mix well. Trim edges from cake. Cut in ½; place on a flat surface. Spread bottom with filling; press other ½ gently on top. Cut cake in 20 slices. Sift cocoa over top. Refrigerate 2 hours. To store, refrigerate in a covered container up to 2 days.

Makes 20 slices.

Grand Marnier Petits Fours

⅓ plain génoise, page 55
GRAND MARNIER CREAM: ¼ cup unsalted butter
3 tablespoons powdered sugar
½ teaspoon grated orange peel
1 egg yolk
1 tablespoon Grand Marnier
ICING: 1 tablespoon light corn syrup
3 tablespoons water
1 tablespoon Grand Marnier
2 cups powdered sugar
yellow food coloring
TO DECORATE: angelica strips

Trim edges of cake and cut into two 10-inch long strips. To make Grand Marnier cream, combine butter, powdered sugar and orange peel in a medium bowl and beat until soft and smooth. Add egg yolk and Grand Marnier in small amounts until thoroughly blended. If mixture separates, place in a bowl set in warm water, and whisk with a fork until smooth. Chill until cream will hold a shape.

Spread top of cake with Grand Marnier cream. Place remaining cream in a piping bag with a star tube and decorate cake. Chill cake until cream is hard. Cut each strip of cake into 10 pieces. Place cakes on a wire rack set over a jelly-roll pan.

To make icing, cook corn syrup and water in a medium saucepan until corn syrup has melted and water is just bubbling. Stir in Grand Marnier and powdered sugar. Remove from heat and beat until smooth. Reheat until tepid. If icing is too thick, add 1 teaspoon of water. Tint icing with yellow food coloring. Spoon icing over cakes. Let stand until icing is set. Decorate with angelica strips.
Makes 20 petits fours.

Nut Cakes with Lemon Syrup

¼ cup (1 oz) ground walnuts
¼ cup (1 oz) ground almonds
1 tablespoon finely-crushed vanilla cookies
grated peel of ½ lemon
1 egg yolk
2 tablespoons superfine sugar
1 egg white
LEMON SYRUP: ¼ cup sugar
1 tablespoon lemon juice
¼ cup (2 fl oz) water
1 tablespoon dark or white rum
TOPPING: ¼ cup (3 oz) apricot jam
2 teaspoons lemon juice
TO DECORATE: walnut pieces or almond flakes

Preheat oven to 350F (180C). Grease 12
miniature tart pans. In a small bowl, mix
nuts with cookie crumbs. Add lemon peel.
In a small bowl, beat egg yolk with sugar
until fluffy. In a small bowl beat egg white
until stiff. Fold into egg yolk mixture. Add
dry ingredients to eggs, ½ at a time. Fold in
gently. Fill tart pans ¾ full of batter. Bake in
preheated oven 15 minutes or until firm.
Cool 2 minutes before soaking with syrup.

To make syrup, in a small saucepan, bring
sugar, lemon juice and water to the boil over
medium heat. Simmer 1 minute. Remove
from heat. Add rum; cool until tepid. Pour
syrup over cakes while still in tart pans. Cool
cakes completely. Carefully run a knife
around edge to remove cake from tart pan.
Place on a wire rack set over a baking sheet.

To make topping, in a small saucepan, heat
the jam and lemon juice. Sieve if lumpy.
Warm before brushing over top of cakes.
Decorate with a walnut piece or almond
flake. Let stand 6 hours. Store covered up to
48 hours.

Makes 12 cakes.

Chocolate Boxes

⅓ chocolate génoise, page 58, cut into 18 squares
7 oz semisweet chocolate, chopped

BUTTER CREAM: 2 teaspoons instant coffee powder
2 teaspoons hot water
¼ cup butter, room temperature
4 tablespoons powdered sugar
1 egg yolk
2 teaspoons brandy or cognac

⅓ cup (4 oz) apricot jam

TO DECORATE: candied violet

Line a baking sheet with waxed paper. Melt chocolate in a bowl or top of a double boiler set over a pan of simmering water. Stir until smooth. Let cool slightly. Spread melted chocolate onto waxed paper to a square 12" x 12". Let set at room temperature.

When set, with a sharp knife, score into 90 squares equivalent to size of cake sides. Cut 18 squares for cake tops. Trim to exact size if necessary. Peel away waxed paper.

To make butter cream, dissolve coffee in hot water in a medium mixing bowl. Cream butter with instant coffee and sugar until soft. Add egg yolk. If mixture curdles, place bowl in warm water. Beat until smooth. Add brandy or cognac. Refrigerate to firm slightly.

Sieve jam and warm in a small saucepan until bubbling. Brush cake tops generously with jam.

Place ¼ teaspoon of butter cream on underside of 4 chocolate pieces. Press 1 chocolate piece on each of the cake's 4 sides. Spoon butter cream into a pastry bag fitted with fluted nozzle. Pipe butter cream along one edge of box.

Place a chocolate lid on top, tilting slightly so cream on one side is visible. Decorate with candied violet. Repeat procedure for remaining 17 boxes. Chill for several hours until firm. Refrigerate boxes up to 24 hours. Remove 1 hour before serving.

Makes 18 boxes.

Miniature Lamingtons

⅓ plain génoise, page 55

ICING: 3 cups powdered sugar
3 tablespoons unsweetened cocoa powder
2 tablespoons butter, melted
warm water
unshredded coconut

Cut génoise into 24 small rectangles.

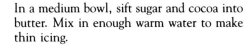

In a medium bowl, sift sugar and cocoa into butter. Mix in enough warm water to make thin icing.

Drop each cake into icing. Turn over to lightly coat on all sides. Remove; place on a wire rack set over a baking sheet. Spoon coconut on top or carefully roll each piece in a small bowl of coconut. Let set. Store in a covered container with waxed paper between layers up to 1 week.

Makes 24 cakes.

Julian's Fruit Cake

3 cups (1lb) pitted dates
²⁄₃ cup mixed citrus peel
²⁄₃ cup red candied cherries
²⁄₃ cup green candied cherries
²⁄₃ cup golden raisins
1½ cups walnuts
¾ cup + 2 tablespoons ground almonds
½ teaspoon baking powder
4 eggs
1 teaspoon cinnamon
½ teaspoon grated nutmeg
2 tablespoons honey
1 to 2 tablespoons whiskey

TO GLAZE: apricot jam, if desired

Preheat oven to 300F (150C). Grease and line a 10″ x 10″ pan with waxed paper. In a large bowl mix fruits and walnuts. Add the almonds, baking powder, eggs, cinnamon, nutmeg, honey and 1 tablespoon of whiskey. Mix well.

Pour into prepared pan. Bake in preheated oven 1 hour or until top is set.

Cool in pan 10 minutes. Brush with remaining whiskey, if desired. Remove from pan; cool completely on a wire rack. Wrap in plastic wrap; let set 48 hours. Cut into 40 small diamonds, squares or strips. To glaze, brush with apricot jam if desired. Refrigerate wrapped up to 1 month.

Makes 40 pieces.

Panforte

1½ cup slivered almonds
1½ cups hazelnuts
⅓ cup (2 oz) glacé cherries, coarsely chopped
⅓ cup (2 oz) mixed citrus peel
½ cup (3 oz) glacé apricots, coarsely chopped
½ cup (3 oz) glacé pineapple, coarsely chopped
3 teaspoons cinnamon
2 rounded tablespoons unsweetened cocoa powder
⅔ cup (3 oz) all-purpose flour
⅔ cup sugar
1 cup (12 oz) honey

Preheat oven to 325F (160C). Grease a 14" x 10" baking pan. Line bottom of pan with parchment paper. Roast almonds and hazelnuts on separate baking sheets in preheated oven. Stir almonds once or twice until golden brown. Roast hazelnuts until skins blister. Wrap hazelnuts in a towel for 1 minute. Rub towel to loosen skins. Coarsely chop nuts. Mix with cherries, peel, apricots, pineapple, cinnamon, cocoa and flour.

Cook sugar and honey in a small saucepan until mixture reaches soft ball stage 234F (112C). Immediately pour syrup over fruit and nuts; mix well. Pour into greased pan. Dampen hands and press mixture to an even thickness.

Bake in preheated oven 30 minutes or until set on the edges. Test top by touching with back of a spoon. Cool in pan on wire rack 10 minutes. Remove from pan and peel off paper. Cool completely on a wire rack. Store in a covered container 1 week before serving.

Makes about 50 pieces.

Brazil Nut Bread

⅓ cup brazil nuts
3 egg whites
pinch of salt
½ cup superfine sugar
¾ cup (3 oz) all-purpose flour
1 teaspoon cinnamon
½ teaspoon nutmeg, freshly ground

Preheat oven to 350F (180C). Grease a 7½″ x 3¾″ loaf pan. Line bottom and sides of pan with waxed paper. Roast brazil nuts on a baking sheet until golden. Remove nuts; wrap in a towel. Let stand 5 minutes. Rub towel until skins are removed.

Beat egg whites with salt until stiff. Add ½ sugar; beat again. When stiff, fold in remaining sugar. Sift flour with spices. Gently fold into egg whites. When partly folded, add nuts. Continue folding until no flour is visible. Spoon mixture into loaf pan and smooth top. Bake in preheated oven 25 to 30 minutes or until top is set. Cool in loaf pan on a wire rack for 10 minutes. Remove from pan and cool completely on wire rack. Peel off paper and wrap in foil. Refrigerate 24 hours or freeze up to 4 to 6 weeks before second baking.

Preheat oven to 300F (150C). Using a serrated knife cut the bread into thin slices. If frozen, partly thaw before slicing. Bake slices on a baking sheet in preheated oven 15 minutes or until golden. Turn slices over and bake 10 to 15 minutes or until crisp. Cool slices on baking sheet. Store in an airtight container up to 3 weeks.

Makes 40 slices.

Almond Orange Bread

2 oranges
1 lemon
3 egg whites
pinch of salt
½ cup superfine sugar
⅔ cup all-purpose flour
½ cup unblanched whole almonds

Remove peel from 1 orange. Place peel in a small saucepan. Cover with cold water. Bring slowly to a boil; drain and rinse under cold running water. Dry on a paper towel. Grate peel of second orange and lemon. Mix with cooked peel.

Preheat oven to 350F (180C). Grease a 7½" x 3¾" loaf pan; line bottom of pan with waxed paper. Beat egg whites with salt until stiff. Add sugar and beat again. Mix in orange and lemon peel. Gently fold in flour. When ½ mixture has been folded, add almonds. Continue folding until no flour remains.

Spoon mixture into loaf pan and smooth top. Bake in preheated oven 35 to 40 minutes or until top is set. Cool in loaf pan on a wire rack 10 minutes. Remove from pan and cool completely on wire rack. Peel off paper and wrap in foil. Refrigerate overnight or freeze up to 4 to 6 weeks before second baking. Preheat oven to 300F (150C). Using a serrated knife, cut bread into thin slices. If frozen partly thaw before slicing. Bake slices on an ungreased baking sheet in preheated oven 15 minutes or until golden. Turn slices over and bake 10 to 15 minutes or until very crisp. Cool slices on baking sheet. Store in an airtight container up to 3 weeks.

Makes 40 slices.

Chocolate Lemon Cheesecakes

FILLING: ½ cup cream cheese, softened
1 egg
2 tablespoons superfine sugar
1 tablespoon lemon juice
CHOCOLATE CAKE: ¾ cup all-purpose flour
½ cup superfine sugar
2 tablespoons unsweetened cocoa powder
½ teaspoon baking soda
½ teaspoon baking powder
pinch of salt
½ cup (4 fl oz) water
2 tablespoons vegetable oil
2 teaspoons lemon juice
1 teaspoon vanilla extract
2 egg yolks
2 egg whites
TO COAT: 2 oz semisweet chocolate
TO DECORATE: Candied violet, if desired

Preheat oven to 350F (180C). Grease bottom and sides of 40 miniature tart pans. Beat cream cheese with egg, sugar and lemon juice until soft and smooth.

Sift flour with sugar, cocoa, soda, baking powder and salt. Add water, oil, lemon juice, vanilla and egg yolks. Beat mixture 30 seconds. In a small bowl, beat egg whites until stiff. Fold into mixture ⅓ at a time. Fill tart pans ½ full of chocolate batter. Drop a teaspoonful of filling in center of each. Bake in preheated oven 12 minutes or until set.

Cool cakes on baking sheet set on wire rack 2 minutes. Carefully run a knife around edge to remove cake from tart pan. Cool on a wire rack. Store in a covered container up to 36 hours. Melt chocolate in a bowl or top of a double boiler set over a pan of simmering water. Invert cakes on a baking sheet. Cover bottom with chocolate. Decorate with candied violet.
Makes 40 cheesecakes.

Frosted Almond Cookies

½ cup butter
grated peel of lemon
½ cup superfine sugar
1 teaspoon vanilla extract
1 cup (4 oz) all-purpose flour
⅓ cup unblanched almonds, ground
2 egg whites
1¼ cups (5 oz) flakes almonds

TO FINISH: powdered sugar

In a medium bowl, cream butter, lemon peel
and sugar until fluffy. Add vanilla and flour.
Mix well to a soft dough. Add almonds.
Chill 1 hour or until firm enough to handle.
Preheat oven to 325F (160C). Grease a
baking sheet.

Roll teaspoonfuls of dough into 50 cylinders.
Flatten to make a log shape. In a small bowl,
whisk egg whites. Dip logs in egg whites,
then in almond flakes. Replace almond
flakes when they become sticky with egg
white.

Place logs close together on prepared baking
sheet. Bake in preheated oven 15 to 20
minutes or until a light golden brown.
Loosen logs from baking sheet. Sift sugar
over top while still warm. Cool on baking
sheet on wire rack. Store in an airtight
container up to 2 weeks.

Makes 50 cookies.

Sugared Hearts

¼ cup butter
½ cup powdered sugar
1 egg yolk
1 teaspoon vanilla extract
⅔ cup (3 oz) all-purpose flour
1 tablespoon finely chopped blanched almonds

TO FINISH: powdered sugar

In a medium bowl, cream butter and sugar until fluffy. Add egg yolk and vanilla; mix in flour. Toast almonds in a dry frying pan until light golden brown, stirring frequently. Cool. Mix almonds into sugar mixture and blend thoroughly. Form into a ball. Chill if sticky.

Preheat oven to 350F (180C). Grease a baking sheet. Roll dough thinly between sheets of waxed paper.

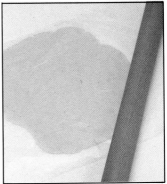

Cut dough into 80 hearts with a small, floured heart cutter. Place hearts on prepared baking sheet. Bake in preheated oven 15 to 20 minutes or until a light golden color. Sift sugar over cookies while still warm. Cool on a wire rack. Store in an airtight container with waxed paper between layers up to 10 days.

Makes 80 hearts.

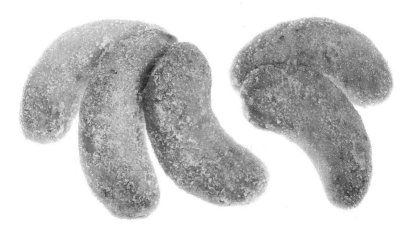

Viennese Almond Crescents

1 cup (4oz) all-purpose flour
2 tablespoons sugar
½ cup butter, cubed
½ cup unblanched almonds
1 egg yolk

TO COAT: superfine sugar

Preheat oven to 350F (180C). Grease a baking sheet. In a medium bowl, sift flour; add sugar. With a pastry blender or 2 knives, cut in butter until mixture resembles coarse crumbs. Mince almonds finely. Add almonds and egg yolk to flour mixture. Knead lightly in bowl until mixture binds well and is sticky. Chill 20 minutes.

Roll 1 teaspoon of pastry into a small log; form a crescent. Repeat. Place crescents close together on prepared baking sheet. Bake in preheated oven 15 minutes or until light golden.

Remove from baking sheet. Spoon sugar over crescents. Cool on a wire rack. Store in an airtight container up to 2 weeks.

Makes 50 cookies.

Iced Cookie Crisps

½ cup self-raising flour
pinch of salt
1 tablespoon superfine sugar
2 tablespoons butter, cubed
1 egg yolk

ICING: ½ cup powdered sugar
1 egg white

TO DECORATE: ¼ cup (1 oz) finely chopped blanched almonds

Grease 2 baking sheets. In a medium bowl, sift flour with salt; add sugar. With a pastry blender or 2 knives, cut in butter until mixture resembles coarse crumbs. Add egg yolk; mix to a paste. Knead lightly in bowl; form into a ball. Wrap and chill dough 30 minutes.

Roll dough between pieces of waxed paper or on a lightly floured surface. Cut dough with a floured 1 inch round cutter. Place cookies on prepared baking sheets.

Preheat oven to 350F (180C). To make icing, beat sugar and egg white together. Place 1 teaspoon icing in center of each cookie. Smooth slightly. Top cookies with almonds. Bake in preheated oven 15 to 18 minutes or until a light golden brown. Remove from baking sheet; cool on a wire rack. Store in an airtight container up to 2 weeks.

Makes 50 cookies.

Glazed Almond Squares

¼ cup butter
½ cup superfine sugar
1 cup ground almonds
2 eggs
2 tablespoons all-purpose flour

TOPPING: ¼ cup butter
⅓ cup (3 oz) sugar
¼ cup (2 fl oz) light corn syrup
¾ cup almond flakes

Preheat oven to 350F (180C). Grease bottom and sides of a 15" x 10" jelly-roll pan. In a medium bowl, cream butter and sugar until light and fluffy. Add ground almonds, eggs and flour and mix well. Spread mixture evenly in prepared jelly-roll pan. Bake in preheated oven 10 minutes until golden.

To make topping, melt butter, sugar and corn syrup in a small saucepan over low heat. Stir in almond flakes. Cook over medium heat 2 minutes. Pour topping over baked cookie layer; smooth evenly.

Bake 5 to 8 minutes until golden brown. Cool in pan on wire rack 10 minutes. Cut into 2½-inch squares. Cool completely in pan or wire rack. Store in an airtight container up to 1 week.

Makes 50 squares.

Chocolate Chip Bars

½ cup butter
½ cup (3 oz) light brown sugar
1 teaspoon vanilla extract
pinch of salt
1 cup (4 oz) all-purpose flour
3½ oz semisweet chocolate pieces
½ cup (2 oz) finely chopped walnuts

Preheat oven to 350F (180C). Grease 11" x 7" baking pan. In a medium bowl cream butter with sugar until fluffy. Add vanilla and mix. Sift salt and flour; add to sugar mixture. Fold in chocolate pieces and walnuts.

Divide mixture and press evenly in prepared pan. Bake in preheated oven 15 to 18 minutes.

Remove from pan ; cool on a wire rack. When cold, cut into 60 bars. Store in airtight container up to 2 weeks.

Makes 60 bars.

Palmiers

6 oz puff pastry
superfine sugar

Grease 2 baking sheets. On a sugared surface, roll puff pastry to a long 18″ x 12″ rectangle. Divide into 2 sections, 9″ x 6″. Fold like a letter. Folding one side; place second side on top. Flatten slightly.

Fold sides to center. Press down firmly; chill.

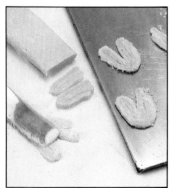

With a very sharp knife, cut 40 thin slices. Dip a flexible spatula in sugar. Press on puff pastry slice to flatten. With a rolling pin, roll very thin. Place cookies about 1 inch apart on prepared baking sheets. Refrigerate 30 minutes. They may be frozen at this stage and baked later without thawing. Preheat oven to 425F (220C). Bake in a preheated oven 5 minutes or until golden. Using a spatula, turn cookies over. Bake until golden. Remove from baking sheets; cool on a wire rack. Store in an airtight container up to 2 weeks.

Makes 40 cookies.

Cigarettes Russes

2 large egg whites
½ cup superfine sugar
⅓ cup butter, melted
1 teaspoon vanilla extract
½ cup (2½ oz) all-purpose flour

Preheat oven to 375F (190C). Grease and flour 2 baking sheets. Shake off excess flour. In a medium bowl, beat egg whites with sugar until smooth. Add butter and vanilla. Mix in flour.

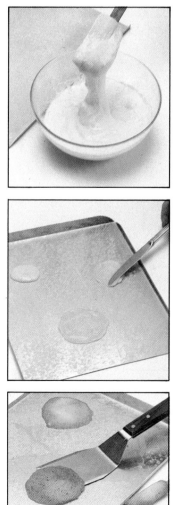

Drop a teaspoonful of mixture on prepared baking sheet. Using a knife, spread mixture thinly and evenly to form a circle 4 inches in diameter. Make only 2 or 3 Cigarettes at a time as they need to be rolled quickly while warm and it is difficult to handle more than this. Bake in preheated oven 5–6 minutes or until golden brown.

Using a spatula, remove cookie from baking sheet. Roll immediately around handle of a wooden spoon. Cigarettes will firm immediately. Cool on a wire rack until crisp. Store in an airtight cake container up to 1 week.

Makes 32 cookies.

Orange Buttons

½ cup blanched almonds, finely chopped
¼ cup + 2 tablespoons mixed citrus peel, finely
  chopped
⅓ cup all-purpose flour
¼ cup butter, cubed
⅓ cup superfine sugar

Preheat oven to 350F (180C). Grease a
baking sheet. In a medium bowl, mix
almonds and peel. Add flour. In another
bowl, cream butter with sugar until fluffy.
Mix almond mixture into sugar mixture;
blend well. Drop by teaspoonfuls on
prepared baking sheet.

Flatten gently with a fork. Bake in preheated
oven 8 to 10 minutes or until cookies are
light golden brown and just set.

Cool on baking sheet on a wire rack 2
minutes. Remove from baking sheet. Cool
completely on wire rack. Store in an airtight
container.

Makes 40 cookies.

Butter Fingers

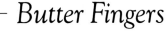

2 tablespoons butter, cubed
1 ½ tablespoons superfine sugar
2 teaspoons whipping cream
1 egg yolk
½ cup all-purpose flour
¼ teaspoon baking powder
1 teaspoon vanilla extract

TO FINISH: 1 ½ oz semisweet or milk chocolate,
chopped

Preheat oven to 325F (160C). Grease a
baking sheet. In a medium mixing bowl,
cream butter and sugar until fluffy; add
cream. Mix in egg yolk. Sift in flour with
baking powder; add vanilla. Mix well.

Spoon mixture into a pastry bag fitted with a
large fluted nozzle. Pipe 40 strips onto
prepared baking sheet. Bake in preheated
oven 15 to 20 minutes or until light golden
brown and firmly set. Cool on baking sheet
or wire rack 1 minute. Remove cookies from
baking sheet; cool on wire racks.

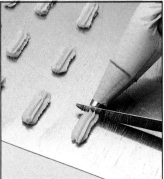

Melt chocolate in a bowl or top of a double
boiler set over a pan of simmering water. Stir
until smooth. Dip both ends of each cookie
into chocolate. Let stand on wire rack until
set. Store in an airtight container up to 10
days.

Makes 40 cookies.

Florentines

1 tablespoon finely chopped blanched almonds
1 tablespoon finely chopped walnuts
1 tablespoon finely chopped glacé cherries
1½ tablespoons chopped mixed citrus peel
4 tablespoons brown sugar
2 tablespoons all-purpose flour
3 tablespoons butter, cubed
3 oz semisweet chocolate, chopped

Preheat oven to 350F (180C). Grease 2 baking sheets. In a medium bowl, mix almonds, walnuts, cherries and citrus peel. In a small bowl, mix sugar with flour. With a pastry blender or 2 knives, cut in butter until mixture resembles coarse crumbs. Add sugar mixture to fruit; mix well. Drop mixture by teaspoonsfuls about 2½ inches apart on prepared baking sheets. Flatten top of each Florentine.

Bake in preheated oven 8 minutes or until golden. Use a palette knife to create rounds. Cool on baking sheets on wire racks until firm. Remove cookies from baking sheets; cool completely on wire racks.

Melt chocolate in a bowl or top of a double boiler set over a pan of simmering water. Stir until smooth. Spread chocolate over flat side of cookies, making wavy lines in chocolate with a fork. Let stand until chocolate is set. Refrigerate in an airtight container up to 1 month.

Makes 25 cookies.

Chocolate Butter Crisps

½ cup all-purpose flour
½ cup self-raising flour
pinch of salt
2 tablespoons unsweetened cocoa powder
½ cup butter
¾ cup powdered sugar
powdered sugar

In a medium bowl, sift flours with salt and cocoa. In another bowl, cream butter and sugar until light. Add sifted, dry ingredients; mix well. Chill 20 minutes.

Preheat oven to 350F (180C). Grease a baking sheet. Form mixture into 60 small balls about size of a cherry. Place on prepared baking sheet.

Press with a fork dipped in powdered sugar. Bake in preheated oven 8 to 10 minutes. Remove from baking sheet; cool on a wire rack. Store in an airtight tin up to 2 weeks.

Makes 60 cookies.

Lattice Jam Cookies

1½ cups (6 oz) all-purpose flour
½ teaspoon baking powder
pinch of salt
½ cup (4oz) butter, cubed
½ cup (4oz) superfine sugar
1 egg yolk
1 teaspoon vanilla extract
½ cup (5 oz) raspberry or apricot jam

Grease baking sheet. In a medium bowl, sift flour with baking powder and salt. Tip the flour mixture into a food processor or use a pastry blender or 2 knives, cut in butter until mixture resembles coarse crumbs. Add sugar, egg yolk and vanilla. Mix to a paste. Knead in bowl 5 seconds until mixture holds together. Divide dough; wrap each ½ in plastic wrap. Chill for 1 hour or until firm.

On a flat surface, roll 1 section of cookie dough to 16″ x 8″. Place on prepared baking sheet. Spread top with jam. Roll out remaining section of cookie dough; cut into strips. Criss-cross strips over jam to form a lattice. Chill 20 minutes.

Preheat oven to 350F (180C). Bake in preheated oven 25 minutes or until golden. Loosen cookie from baking sheet. Cool completely on a wire rack. Cut cookie into 50 pieces. Store in an airtight container up to 10 days.

Makes 50 pieces.

Almond Cookies

1 egg
1¼ cup powdered sugar
grated peel of 1 lemon
1 teaspoon vanilla extract
1⅔ cup ground almonds
1 teaspoon baking powder

TO DECORATE: almond slivers

Line 2 baking sheets with parchment paper. In a medium bowl, beat egg with sugar 3 minutes. Add lemon peel and vanilla. Mix in ground almonds and baking powder; stir well.

Dampen plastic wrap. Place mixture on plastic wrap. Form into a 16 inch roll. Freeze 1 hour.

Preheat oven to 350F (180C). Cut dough into thin slices. Space on parchment-lined baking sheets. Return dough to freezer. Decorate slices with almond slivers. Bake in a preheated oven 15 minutes or until golden. Cool on baking sheets on wire racks 2 minutes or until crisp. Peel cookies off paper; cool on wire racks. Repeat procedure with remaining dough. Store in an airtight container up to 2 weeks.

Makes 100 cookies.

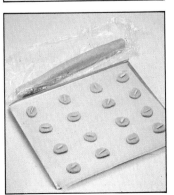

Pistachio Wafers

¼ cup butter, cubed
½ cup superfine sugar
1 teaspoon vanilla extract
2 egg whites
½ cup (2 oz) all-purpose flour
¼ cup pistachio nuts

In a medium bowl, cream butter and sugar until light and fluffy. Add vanilla. In a small bowl, beat egg whites until frothy. Using whisk, gradually add egg whites to sugar mixture. Sift in ⅓ flour; stir well. Repeat twice with remaining flour. Let stand 10 minutes. In a small bowl, cover nuts with boiling water. Let stand until water is tepid. Remove skins; chop nuts finely.

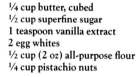

Preheat oven to 350F (180C). Grease 2 baking sheets. Drop teaspoonfuls of wafer mixture about 3½ inches apart on prepared baking sheets. Using a knife, spread wafers to a thin circle 3 inches in diameter. Sprinkle nuts on top.

Bake in preheated oven 10 minutes or until wafers are pale brown. Remove wafers; place over a rolling pin to curve slightly. Cool on a wire rack. Repeat procedure with remaining dough. Store in an airtight container up to 2 weeks.

Makes 30 wafers.

Coconut Fruit Strips

4 oz semisweet chocolate, chopped
⅓ cup butter, melted, cooled
2 eggs, lightly beaten
1 cup superfine sugar
2 cups shredded coconut
4 tablespoons finely chopped glacé ginger, cherries or apricots

Line a jelly-roll pan with foil; grease foil. Melt chocolate in a bowl or top of a double boiler set over a pan of simmering water. Stir until smooth. Pour chocolate into jelly-roll pan; smooth out with metal spatula to form a smooth, thin layer. Chill 20 minutes or until firm.

Preheat oven to 350F (180C). Add butter gradually to eggs, mixing well. Stir in sugar and coconut. Add fruit pieces. Beat for 10 seconds. Spoon mixture over chocolate base and spread evenly.

Bake in preheated oven 25 minutes or until top is golden brown and firm to touch. Remove and cool 4 hours or until chocolate base is set. Remove from pan. Invert and peel off foil. Invert again and cut into small squares. Store in an airtight container up to 1 week.

Makes 60 pieces.

Rocky Road Cookies

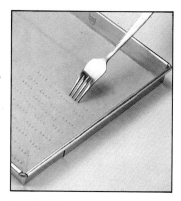

BISCUIT CRUST: 1 cup (4 oz) all-purpose flour
pinch of salt
⅓ cup butter, chopped
2 tablespoons powdered sugar
1 egg yolk

TOPPING: 1 tablespoon whipping cream
1¼ cups marshmallows
½ cup (2½ oz) chopped, dry-roasted, unsalted peanuts
2 tablespoons glacé cherries, coarsely chopped

CHOCOLATE COATING: 3 oz semisweet chocolate, chopped
2 tablespoons butter

Grease a 10″ x 10″ baking pan. In a medium bowl, sift flour and salt. With a pastry blender or 2 knives, cut in butter until mixture resembles coarse crumbs. Add sugar and egg yolk. Mix to a dough. Roll dough between waxed paper. Press to fit prepared pan in an even layer. Prick top and chill for 20 minutes. Preheat oven to 350F (180C). Bake 15 to 20 minutes or until a light golden color. Remove and cool on a wire rack.

To make topping, heat cream in a small saucepan. Add marshmallows and melt over low heat. Add nuts and cherries. Smooth marshmallow mixture evenly over biscuit crust. Let set.

Melt butter and chocolate, in top of a double boiler set over a pan of simmering water. Stir occasionally. Spread chocolate over marshmallow. Make fork marks on the top in a decorative pattern. Let set. Wrap and store up to 1 week in the refrigerator. To serve, cut pieces as needed.

Makes about 45 pieces.

Chocolate Cinnamon Wafers

¼ cup light brown sugar
¼ cup superfine sugar
3 egg whites
1 tablespoon and 2 teaspoons all-purpose flour
1 tablespoon and 2 teaspoons unsweetened cocoa powder
pinch of salt
½ teaspoon cinnamon
2 tablespoons whipping cream
2 tablespoons butter, melted

Preheat oven to 350F (180C). Grease and flour 2 baking sheets. Shake out excess flour. In a medium bowl, combine sugars and egg whites; whisk. Sift flour, cocoa, salt, and cinnamon into sugar mixture. Add the cream and butter; mix well.

Drop 2 teaspoons of mixture on prepared baking sheets. Using a knife, spread to make a thin even circle about 4 inches in diameter. Repeat procedure; each baking sheet will hold 4 wafers. Bake in a preheated oven 8 minutes. Test for doneness by lightly touching wafer. No imprint should remain if done.

Remove wafers from baking sheets. Place over a rolling pin, pressing gently to curve. When crisp, cool on a rack. Repeat procedure with remaining batter. Store within 1 hour in an airtight container up to 10 days.

Makes 30 wafers.

Brandy Snaps

⅓ cup butter, cubed
3 tablespoons light corn syrup
⅓ cup firmly-packed light brown sugar
½ teaspoon grated fresh ginger
1 teaspoon ground ginger
½ cup all-purpose flour

Preheat oven to 350F (180C). Grease a baking sheet. In a small saucepan, cook butter, corn syrup and brown sugar over low heat until butter melts. Stir occasionally. Add fresh and ground ginger. Remove from heat. Sift flour into a medium bowl. Mix liquid into flour; stir well.

Drop a teaspoonful of mixture about 2 inches apart on prepared baking sheet. Bake in preheated oven 5 to 7 minutes or until golden brown.

Loosen brandy snaps with a spatula. Cool 5 seconds. Roll each cookie smooth side outwards around handle of a wooden spoon. Cool completely on a wire rack. Repeat with remaining cookies. Store in an airtight container up to 10 days. To serve, fill with whipped cream or Orange Cream Filling, page 90.

Makes 30 small cookies.

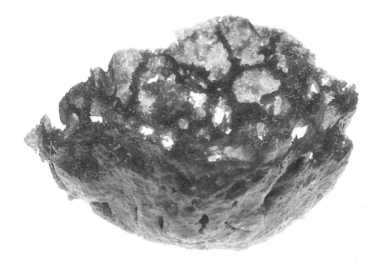

Brandy Snap Baskets

¹⁄₃ cup butter, cubed
3 tablespoons light corn syrup
¹⁄₃ cup firmly-packed light brown sugar
¹⁄₂ teaspoon ground ginger
1 teaspoon ground ginger
¹⁄₂ cup all-purpose flour

Preheat oven to 350F (180C). Grease a baking sheet. In a small saucepan, cook butter, with corn syrup and brown sugar over low heat until butter melts. Stir occasionally. Add fresh and ground ginger. Remove from heat. Sift flour into a medium bowl. Mix liquid into flour; stir well.

Drop a teaspoonful of mixture about 2 inches apart on prepared baking sheet. Bake in preheated oven 5 to 7 minutes or until golden brown.

To make a basket, remove 1 cookie from sheet and place over a tiny inverted coffee cup, measuring cup or egg cup 2 seconds. Gently squeeze sides into shape. Cool on a wire rack. Repeat with remaining cookies. Store in an airtight container 10 days. To serve, fill with whipped cream or Orange Cream Filling, page 90, and fresh fruit.

Makes 30 baskets.

Orange Cream Filling

1 cup whipping cream
grated peel of 1 medium orange
2 tablespoons powdered sugar
1 tablespoon orange liqueur

TO DECORATE: **fresh strawberries or raspberries**

In a small bowl, whip cream until soft peaks form. Add orange peel. Sift sugar over top. Mix well; add liqueur. Chill 2 hours.

Spoon filling into a pastry bag fitted with an open star tip. If using filling for brandy snaps, pipe a small amount of filling into each end.

If filling baskets, pipe a small amount of filling in center. To decorate, halve strawberries; remove green hull. Place ½ a strawberry in a basket. If using raspberries, place a raspberry, and a tiny piece of mint leaf in center of each basket. Serve immediately.

Makes 30 cookies.

Chocolate Almond Crisps

1 ½ cups (6 oz) ground almonds
½ cup superfine sugar
pinch of salt
2 oz semisweet chocolate, chopped
3 egg whites
1 teaspoon vanilla extract

Preheat oven to 325F (160C). Line a baking
sheet with parchment paper. Toast almonds
in a dry frying pan until golden brown. Stir
occasionally. Remove pan from heat. Stir in
sugar and salt.

Melt chocolate in a bowl or top of a double
boiler set over a pan of simmering water. Stir
until smooth. In a medium bowl, stir
chocolate into almond mixture. Add 2 egg
whites to form a paste. Add vanilla. In a
bowl, beat remaining egg white until stiff.
Fold through mixture, ⅓ at a time.

Drop teaspoonfuls of mixture 1 inch apart on
lined baking sheets. Bake in preheated oven
25 to 30 minutes or until set. Cool on
baking sheet on wire rack 5 minutes.
Remove from baking sheet; cool on wire
rack. Store in an airtight container up to 2
weeks.

Makes 60 cookies.

Butter Pastry Tart Cups

1 cup all-purpose flour
pinch of salt
⅓ cup butter, cubed
2 teaspoons powdered sugar
1 tablespoon lemon juice

In a medium bowl, sift flour with salt. Place butter in center of flour. Add sugar and lemon juice. Stir with end of a blunt knife to make a soft, lumpy dough. Do not use a fork or dough will not be right consistency. Knead in bowl 8 to 10 strokes or until dough binds together. Form pastry into a ball. Wrap in plastic wrap; refrigerate 20 minutes until firm or freeze.

Preheat oven to 350F (180C). Grease 48 miniature tart pans. Roll ½ of pastry very thinly between 2 layers of waxed paper. Using a tart pan as a cutter, press into pastry. Line tart pan with pastry circle. Repeat procedure for remaining tart pans. Refrigerate 20 minutes or until firm.

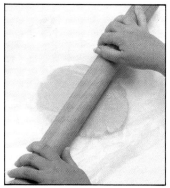

Prick pastry with poultry skewer. Line pastry with foil. Arrange tart cups on baking sheets. Bake in preheated oven 8 to 10 minutes or until set. Remove foil. Bake 3 minutes until light golden brown. To fill, see pages 97, 99, 100.

Makes 48 tart cups.

Miniature Tarts

1 cup all-purpose flour
pinch of salt
¼ cup ground almonds
⅓ cup butter, cubed
½ cup powdered sugar
1 egg yolk
1 teaspoon vanilla extract

On a flat surface, sift flour and salt. Sprinkle ground almonds on top. Make an indentation in center. Place butter, sugar, egg yolk and vanilla extract in indentation. Using fingers, work butter sugar and egg yolk with vanilla. When partly blended, work in flour gradually from outside edges to form a paste. Knead gently 1 minute. Shape pastry into a flattened ball. Wrap in waxed paper; chill 2 hours. To freeze, wrap in plastic wrap. Thaw in refrigerator before using.

Preheat oven to 325F (170C). Grease 3 baking sheets. Unwrap pastry and divide in ½. Roll to a thin layer between 2 sheets of waxed paper. Cut dough into 20 rounds with a floured 1-inch cutter. Arrange circles on prepared baking sheets. Repeat procedure with remaining ½ of dough.

With remaining pastry, form a thin strip shaped like a sausage. Place around pastry circle to form a ridge. Prick base with a fork. Repeat procedure for each tart. Bake in preheated oven 15 to 18 minutes or until golden. Cool on baking sheets or wire racks 2 minutes. Remove from baking sheets; cool on wire racks. Store up to 1 month. To crisp, bake at 350F (180C) 2 minutes. To fill, see pages 94, 95, 96.

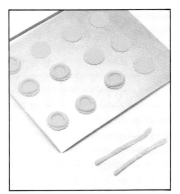

Makes 40 tarts.

Cream Cheese Tarts

18 miniature tarts, page 93

FILLING: ¼ cup (2 oz) cream cheese
½ teaspoon grated orange peel
1 tablespoon powdered sugar

TOPPING: 9 large strawberries, 36 fresh raspberries or
    2 kiwi fruit, sliced
2 tablespoons redcurrant jelly or apricot jam

To make filling, cream cheese with orange peel and sugar in a small bowl until soft.

Place about ½ teaspoon of filling in center of each tart. Refrigerate up to 8 hours. Before serving, arrange fruit and jam or jelly on top. If using strawberries, cut in ½. Leave a piece of green stem on each ½. Place ½ a strawberry or a few raspberries on top of each tart. Or top each tart with a slice of kiwi fruit.

If using berries, melt redcurrant jelly in a small saucepan until thin. Use apricot jam with kiwi fruit. Using a small pastry brush, dab jelly or jam on fruit. Chill before serving.

Makes 18 tarts.

Chocolate Liqueur Tarts

24 miniature tarts, page 93

CHOCOLATE FILLING: 9½ oz milk chocolate, chopped
1 tablespoon light corn syrup
½ cup (4 fl oz) whipping cream
2 tablespoons orange liqueur, cognac or whiskey

TO DECORATE: whipped cream
candied violet

Grate or chop chocolate.

In a small saucepan, bring corn syrup and cream to a boil. Add chocolate; and remove from heat. Let stand for 2 minutes. Stir until chocolate melts. Add liqueur, cognac or whiskey. Stir well; cool.

Refrigerate in a covered container up to 6 weeks. Warm slightly before filling tarts. Leave to set before serving. Decorate each tart with whipped cream and small piece of candied violet. Serve within 4 hours.

Makes 24 tarts.

Lemon Butter Tarts

12 miniature tarts, page 93

LEMON BUTTER FILLING: 2 eggs
1 cup (7 oz) superfine sugar
grated peel of 2 medium lemons
½ cup (4 fl oz) lemon juice
3 tablespoons (1½ oz) butter, cubed

TO DECORATE: mixed citrus peel
          mint leaves

In a bowl or top of a double boiler, beat eggs and sugar until fluffy.

Add lemon peel, lemon juice and butter. Place bowl or top of double boiler over a pan of boiling water and cook, stirring until thick. Cool; stir occasionally. Refrigerate in a dry, sterilized container up to 4 weeks. Makes 2 cups of mixture.

To serve, use a spoon to fill each tart with lemon butter mixture. Decorate each tart with a small piece of citrus peel and a mint leaf. Store remaining filling in container in refrigerator and use as required.

Makes 12 tarts.

Citrus Soufflé Tarts

30 butter pastry tart cups, page 92

CITRUS SOUFFLÉ: 1 egg yolk
2 tablespoons superfine sugar
grated peel of 1 medium orange
1 tablespoon lemon juice
1 teaspoon cornstarch
2 tablespoons orange juice
1 large egg white
1 tablespoon sugar

Preheat oven to 350F (180C). In a small saucepan, whisk egg yolk, sugar, orange peel and lemon juice. In a small bowl, mix cornstarch with 1 tablespoon orange juice. Add remaining orange juice; stir into egg yolk mixture. Whisk gently over high heat to thicken evenly. Do not boil. Pour into a small bowl; cool.

In a small bowl, beat egg white until stiff. Add sugar; beat until stiff and glossy. Fold egg white into citrus mixture, ½ at a time.

Using a teaspoon form a mound of filling in each tart cup; smooth top. Arrange tarts on baking sheet. Bake in preheated oven 10 minutes or until firm and light golden brown. Cool on baking sheet or wire rack 5 minutes. Remove from tart pans carefully while still warm. Cool on a wire rack. Store uncovered up to 36 hours.

Makes 30 tarts.

Miniature Swiss Tarts

¾ cup all-purpose flour
pinch of salt
½ cup butter
2 tablespoons superfine sugar
1 teaspoon vanilla extract

TO FINISH: redcurrant jelly
powdered sugar

Preheat oven to 350F (180C). In a small bowl, sift flour and salt. In a medium bowl, cream butter with sugar until light and fluffy. Add vanilla extract. Add flour mixture ½ at a time. Beat mixture 2 minutes or until soft.

Spoon dough into a pastry bag fitted with a fluted nozzle. Pipe small rings, leaving indentation in centers, into paper cases set on a baking sheet. Bake in preheated oven 12 to 15 minutes or until light golden brown. Cool on baking sheet on a wire rack.

Fill tart cavity with redcurrant jelly. Sift sugar lightly over tarts. Store in an airtight container in a single layer up to 10 days.

Makes 60 tarts.

Almond Tarts

24 butter pastry tart cups, page 92, warmed

ALMOND FILLING: 2 tablespoons butter, cubed
2 tablespoons superfine sugar
¼ cup ground almonds
1 drop almond extract
1 egg yolk
1 teaspoon whipping cream
1 teaspoon brandy

¼ cup apricot jam
1 teaspoon lemon juice
24 slivered almonds

Preheat oven to 350F (180C). With a fork, cream butter. Add sugar; mix until light and fluffy. Add almonds, almond extract, egg yolk, cream, and brandy. Mix thoroughly.

In a small saucepan, warm jam and lemon juice. If lumpy, sieve or chop apricot pieces finely. Arrange tart cups on a baking sheet. Place a small dab of apricot jam in each tart cup.

Fill each tart cup with almond filling. Top with an almond sliver. Bake in preheated oven 10 minutes or until set. Cool on baking sheet on a wire rack 1 minute. Run a knife around each tart edge. Cool on a wire rack. The rich flavor of these tarts will mature if they are kept for 12 hours before serving. Store up to 2 days.

Makes 24 tarts.

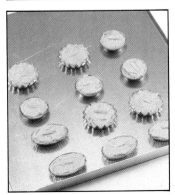

Chocolate Almond Tarts

25 butter pastry tart cups, page 92

CHOCOLATE ALMOND FILLING: 1 egg
½ cup superfine sugar
2 tablespoons unsweetened cocoa powder
½ cup ground almonds
3 tablespoons whipping cream

TO DECORATE: flaked almonds

To make filling, whisk egg and sugar until warm and lightly thickened in a heatproof bowl set over a pan of warm water. Remove bowl from pan.

Add cocoa, almonds and cream. Mix well; cool. Refrigerate up to 24 hours.

Preheat oven to 350F (180C). Arrange tart cups on a baking sheet. Fill tart cups with filling. Decorate with almond flakes. Bake in preheated oven 8 to 10 minutes or until puffed on top and firm to touch. Cool on baking sheet on wire rack 1 minute. Remove from sheet and cool on a wire rack. Serve within 36 hours.

Makes 25 tarts.

Cream Puffs

½ cup all-purpose flour
pinch of salt
½ cup cold water
¼ cup butter, cubed
3 eggs

Preheat oven to 425F (220C). Grease and lightly flour 2 baking sheets. Shake off excess flour. Sift flour and salt onto waxed paper. In a small saucepan bring butter and water to boil over low heat. Butter should melt by time liquid bubbles. Remove from heat. Using waxed paper as a chute, add flour. Stir immediately with a wooden spoon. Mixture will thicken and form a ball in pan. Transfer to a medium bowl.

In a small bowl, beat 3 eggs with a wooden spoon. Gradually add 2 eggs, beating well between each addition, until mixture is glossy and thick.

To make puffs, spoon mixture into a pastry bag fitted with a plain nozzle ½ inch in diameter. Pipe 50 puffs 1 inch in diameter onto prepared baking sheets. Release pressure before lifting bag. If making éclairs, pipe 1½" lengths. Glaze top of each puff with remaining egg. Bake in preheated oven 12 minutes. Adjust temperature to 350F (180C); bake 10 minutes until the puffs are firm to touch and golden brown. Remove puffs from baking sheets. Pierce side of each puff with a small sharp knife. Turn off oven; open door. Place puffs in oven 10 minutes to dry completely; cool. Refrigerate in covered container up to 1 week or freeze wrapped up to 1 month. Crisp by baking at 350F (180C) 5 minutes. To serve, see pages 102, 103, 104, 105.
Makes 50 puffs.

Coffee Cream Puffs

18 cream puffs, page 101

FILLING: 1 cup milk
1 egg
1 tablespoon all-purpose flour
1 tablespoon cornstarch
2 tablespoons sugar
1 teaspoon vanilla extract
2 teaspoons brandy or cognac
1 teaspoon instant coffee powder
1 teaspoon hot water
2 tablespoons whipping cream, whipped

ICING: 1 tablespoon cream
1 teaspoon instant coffee powder
½ cup powdered sugar

In a small saucepan, heat milk until almost boiling. In a medium bowl, beat egg with flour, cornstarch and sugar. Gradually whisk milk into egg mixture. Return mixture to pan. Cook, stirring constantly 2 minutes or until mixture thickens and comes to a boil. Remove from heat; add vanilla and brandy or cognac. In a small bowl, dissolve coffee powder in hot water. Mix into hot mixture. Cool until firm. Fold in cream. Chill until thick. Filling can be frozen up to 1 month. Thaw at room temperature; stir to smooth.

Cut a small slit in side of each puff. Spoon filling into a pastry bag fitted with a plain nozzle. Fill each puff through slit. Or cut each puff in ½. Spoon filling onto bottom; replace top.

Heat cream and coffee powder until bubbling. Remove from heat. Add sugar; stir until smooth. Cook until tepid. Pour or spoon icing on top of each filled puff. Refrigerate. Eat within a few hours.

Makes 18 puffs.

Caramel Puffs

18 cream puffs, page 101
1 recipe of filling without instant coffee powder,
  page 102

CARAMEL TOPPING: ½ cup sugar
4 tablespoons water

Stir filling until smooth. Cut each puff in ½; spoon filling onto bottom; replace top. Or cut a small slit in side of each puff. Spoon filling into a pastry bag fitted with a plain nozzle. Fill each puff.

Grease a wire rack and baking sheet. Place wire rack over baking sheet. Arrange puffs on wire rack. To make topping, in a small saucepan, cook sugar and water over low heat. Shake pan occasionally until sugar dissolves. Adjust heat to medium. Cook rapidly until mixture is a light golden brown. Using a pastry brush dipped in cold water, remove sugar crystals from sides of pan.

Using a long-handled spoon, coat top of each puff with topping. Repeat process if top is not well covered. Let stand 10 minutes or until caramel is firm. Using a small knife, remove puffs from wire rack. Refrigerate up to 12 hours.

Makes 18 puffs.

Eclairs

18 éclairs, made from cream puff paste, page 101

FILLING: ½ cup (4 fl oz) whipping cream, whipped
¼ teaspoon vanilla extract

ICING: 1 tablespoon butter
1 oz semisweet chocolate, chopped
1 tablespoon whipping cream
½ cup powdered sugar
warm water

In a small bowl, mix cream and vanilla.

Cut a small slit in one end of each éclair. Spoon cream into a pastry bag fitted with a plain nozzle. Fill each éclair with cream. Or cut each éclair in ½. Spoon or pipe cream onto bottom; replace top.

To make icing, in a small saucepan, combine butter, chocolate and cream. Cook over low heat until chocolate melts. Add sugar; mix well. Stir in a small amount of warm water until icing is smooth. Coat tops of éclairs with chocolate icing. Serve immediately.

Makes 18 éclairs.

Praline and Orange Puffs

18 cream puffs baked with topping of finely-chopped
almonds, page 101

FILLING: ½ cup whipping cream, whipped
1 tablespoon powdered sugar
1 teaspoon vanilla extract
grated peel of an orange
2 tablespoons finely crushed almond praline, page 29

TO FINISH: powdered sugar

In a small bowl, mix cream, sugar, vanilla
and orange peel. Stir in praline, evenly.

Cut each puff ⅔ from bottom leaving ⅓ for
a cap. Spoon filling into each puff and
replace lid.

To coat, sift sugar over puffs and chill 1 hour
before serving. Refrigerate up to 12 hours.

Makes 18 puffs.

Meringue Crunchies

1 egg white
pinch of salt
⅓ cup sugar
¾ cup (1 oz) crushed cornflakes
2 oz semisweet chocolate, grated

Preheat oven to 325F (160C). Grease a baking sheet. In a small mixing bowl, beat egg white with salt until stiff. Gradually add sugar and beat to a stiff meringue.

In a separate bowl, mix cornflakes and chocolate. Fold into meringue.

Drop teaspoonfuls of mixture on greased baking sheet. Bake in preheated oven 20 minutes or until firm to touch. Remove from baking sheet; cool completely on a wire rack to crisp. Store in an airtight container up to 3 weeks.

Makes 50 crunchies.

Surprise Meringues

⅓ cup pitted dates, finely chopped
grated peel of ½ orange
2 teaspoons chopped mixed citrus peel
2 tablespoons finely chopped pecans
1 tablespoon orange juice
2 teaspoons orange liqueur
1 egg white
2 tablespoons superfine sugar

In a small saucepan, cook dates, orange peel, mixed citrus peel, nuts, orange juice and liqueur. Cook over low heat for 2 minutes or until mixture is hot and dates have softened slightly. Remove from heat and cool mixture. Form mixture into 12 small balls. Let dry for 2 hours.

Preheat oven to 325F (160C). Grease a baking sheet. In a small mixing bowl, beat egg white until stiff. Add sugar and beat until a stiff meringue is formed. Using a tooth pick, dip balls into meringue, one at a time, evenly coating. Space meringues on baking sheet. Remove tooth pick, using a second pick as a lever.

Bake in preheated oven 25 minutes or until golden and firm to touch. Remove from baking sheet; cool completely on wire rack. Serve within 6 hours, or the meringues will soften. However, if left for 24 hours they will dry again.

Makes 12 meringues.

Mushroom Meringues

2 egg whites
pinch of salt
¼ teaspoon cream of tartar
⅓ cup superfine sugar
1 teaspoon vanilla extract
unsweetened cocoa powder, sifted

FILLING: ½ cup (4 fl oz) whipping cream
1 oz milk chocolate, chopped
2 teaspoons brandy

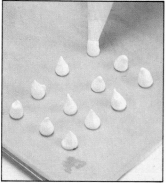

Preheat oven to 300F (150C). Line 2 baking sheets with parchment paper. In a small mixing bowl, beat egg whites with salt and cream of tartar until stiff. Gradually add sugar and vanilla extract and beat to a very stiff meringue. To form caps, spoon ⅔ meringue into a pastry bag fitted with a plain nozzle. Pipe 40 small mounds onto paper-lined baking sheet. Dust tops with cocoa.

Spoon remaining meringue into a pastry bag fitted with a plain nozzle. Pipe 40 mushroom stalks on second paper-lined baking sheet. Bake meringues in preheated oven 10 minutes. Adjust oven temperature to 250F (120C). Bake stalks 1–1½ hours, caps 1½–2 hours until very crisp. Cool on baking sheets on wire racks. Remove cooled meringues from paper. Store in an airtight container.

To make filling, warm cream in a small saucepan. Add chocolate to cream; stir until melted. Add brandy; cool mixture before refrigerating. When mixture is completely cold, whisk gently until soft peaks form. Place filling in bottom of each meringue cap and insert a stalk. Serve immediately.

Makes 40 mushrooms.

Coffee Meringues

2 egg whites
½ cup powdered sugar
2 teaspoons instant coffee powder
2 teaspoons hot water

FILLING: ⅓ cup (2½ fl oz) whipped cream
TO DECORATE: 16 small pieces glacé cherry

Preheat oven to 300F (150C). Line a baking
sheet with parchment paper. Beat egg whites
and sugar in a heatproof bowl over a pan of
simmering water until stiff. Dissolve coffee in
water. Add coffee to meringue and beat.
Remove ¼ cup of meringue; cover and
refrigerate for use as filling.

Drop teaspoonfuls of meringue into 32 small
mounds of similar size on paper-lined baking
sheet. Bake meringues in preheated oven 30
minutes or until crisp. Cool on baking sheet
or wire rack. Carefully remove cooled
meringues from paper. Store in an airtight
container up to 2 weeks.

To make filling mix reserved meringue with
whipped cream; blend well. Store in
refrigerator up to 4 days. To serve, join pairs
of meringues together with filling. Place in
paper cases. To decorate, place a small piece
of glacé cherry on top of cream filling.

Makes 16 petits fours.

Coconut Macaroons

½ cup sugar
¼ cup (2 fl oz) water
2 egg whites
pinch of salt
1¾ cups shredded coconut
1 teaspoon vanilla extract

Preheat oven to 325F (170C). Grease 2 baking sheets. In a small saucepan, cook sugar and water until sugar dissolves. Adjust heat to medium; cook syrup to soft ball stage (234F/115C). Syrup should form a small round ball when dropped into a cup of cold water. In a medium bowl, beat egg whites and salt until stiff. Gradually add sugar syrup. Beat constantly until mixture is thick and glossy.

Add coconut and vanilla. Stir well.

Drop by teaspoonfuls 1 inch apart on prepared baking sheets. Use a wet spatula to even sides. Bake in preheated oven 20 to 25 minutes until crisp and light golden brown. Remove from baking sheets. Cool on a wire rack. Store in an airtight container up to 6 weeks.

Makes 50 macaroons.

Tiny Meringues

2 egg whites
pinch of salt
¼ teaspoon cream of tartar
⅓ cup superfine sugar
1 teaspoon vanilla extract

FILLING: ½ cup whipped cream
blueberries, raspberries, redcurrants or baby
strawberries

TO DECORATE: 30 small pieces of angelica or baby
mint leaves

Preheat oven to 300F (150C). Line a baking
sheet with parchment paper. Beat egg whites
until stiff with salt and cream of tartar. Add
½ sugar and beat again. Add remainder of
sugar and beat until very stiff. Add vanilla.

Form teaspoonfuls of meringue into 30 small
flat buttons on paper-lined baking sheet.
Spoon remaining meringue into small pastry
bag fitted with a small fluted nozzle. Pipe
around edge of circles, keeping well inside
bottom to form a casing.

Bake meringues in preheated oven 10
minutes. Adjust oven temperature to 250F
(120C). Bake until the meringues are crisp
to touch and lightly colored. If meringues
begin to darken, turn oven off and let stand
to crisp. Cool on baking sheet on wire rack.
Carefully remove cooled meringues from
paper. Store in an airtight tin up to 2 weeks.
To fill meringues, spoon cream into a small
pastry bag fitted with a fluted nozzle. Pipe a
small rosette into the center of meringue.
Top with blueberries, raspberries, red
currants or a tiny strawberry. Decorate with
angelica or mint leaves. Serve immediately.

Makes 30 meringues.

Chocolate Nut Fudge

½ cup butter, cubed
¾ cup (6 fl oz) milk
4 tablespoons unsweetened cocoa powder
3⅓ cups sugar
1 teaspoon vanilla extract
½ cup (2 oz) finely chopped pecans or walnuts

Grease a 11" x 7" baking pan. Line bottom with foil.

In a large saucepan, melt butter, add milk. Sift in cocoa; add sugar. Cook over medium heat to dissolve sugar. Shake saucepan rather than stirring mixture. Bring mixture to a boil. Cook until mixture reaches 238F (114C) or until a small piece dropped into cold water forms a soft ball.

Remove from heat. Let cool 5 minutes. Beat with a wooden spoon until thick but still glossy. Add vanilla and nuts. Pour mixture into prepared pan; press down firmly. Let cool 2 hours. To remove fudge from pan, run a knife around edge of pan and invert. Remove foil and cut into 50 pieces. Store in refrigerator in an airtight container up to 4 weeks.

Makes 50 pieces.

Festive Fudge

1 cup (8 fl oz) milk
½ cup butter, cubed
3 cups sugar
1 teaspoon vanilla extract
2 tablespoons finely chopped glacé cherries
2 tablespoons finely chopped glacé ginger
2 tablespoons finely chopped walnuts

Lightly grease an 8½" x 4½" loaf pan. In a small saucepan, bring milk to boil. Add sugar and butter. Cook on low heat uncovered to 240F (116C) or until a soft ball is formed. Use a candy thermometer to maintain an even temperature. Stir occasionally.

Remove from heat and add vanilla, fruit and nuts. For a firm grainy texture, beat immediately with a wooden spoon. For a softer texture, let cool to 115F (50C) before beating.

Pour mixture into prepared greased pan; cool before cutting. For softer fudge, leave 12 hours before cutting. Store in an airtight container up to 3 weeks.

Makes about 50 pieces.

Mocha Coconut Roughs

1⅓ cup shredded coconut
4 oz milk chocolate, chopped
4 oz semisweet chocolate, chopped
2 tablespoons butter, melted
2 teaspoons instant coffee granules

Toast coconut in a dry frying pan. Stir until golden brown. Remove and cool.

Melt milk and semisweet chocolate in a bowl or top of a double boiler set over a pan of simmering water. Stir in butter, coffee and coconut.

Drop by teaspoonfuls onto waxed paper to set. Store for up to 1 month.

Makes 60 pieces.

Marshmallow Chocolate Balls

¼ cup raisins
1 tablespoon brandy
¼ cup butter
3 oz. semisweet chocolate, chopped
1 cup shredded coconut
5 oz marshmallows
2 teaspoons whipping cream

Soak raisins in brandy for 24 hours until brandy has been absorbed and raisins are plump. Melt butter in a small saucepan. Remove from heat and add chocolate. Let stand covered until chocolate has softened. Stir until smooth. Add raisins and brandy. Pour mixture into a medium bowl. Refrigerate until firm enough to form into tiny balls. Chill balls until firm.

Toast coconut in a frying pan. Stir frequently so color is even. Spread on a plate to cool. Combine marshmallows and cream in a bowl or top of a double boiler set over a pan of simmering water. Stir until marshmallows melt. This mixture should be just warm for dipping chocolate balls.

Place a chocolate ball in a teaspoon and dip into marshmallow mixture. Lift immediately. Roll ball in coconut until coated. Marshmallow can be shaped after ball is rolled in coconut. Place on a plate. Continue until all balls are coated. Refrigerate until firm. Store covered with foil between layers in refrigerator.

Makes 24 balls.

Chocolate Torrone

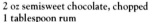

2 oz semisweet chocolate, chopped
1 tablespoon rum
¼ cup butter
1 tablespoon powdered sugar
1 small egg yolk
¼ cup ground almonds
1 egg white
2 tablespoons coarse cookie crumbs

Line miniature pan of 1 cup capacity with foil and grease lightly. Place chocolate and rum in a bowl or top of a double boiler set over a pan of simmering water. Melt and stir until smooth. Let stand until tepid.

Beat butter until creamy. Stir in sugar, egg yolk and ground almonds. Beat chocolate into butter mixture a little at a time. Beat egg white until stiff; fold into chocolate mixture ⅓ at a time. Mix in cookie crumbs.

Spoon mixture in pan and smooth top. Cover with plastic wrap; chill for 6 hours or until firm. To unmold, run a knife around edge and invert Torrone. Slice into 10 pieces and then cut each slice in ½. Refrigerate until served.

Makes 20 pieces.

Chocolate Kirsch Log

4 oz semisweet chocolate
½ cup finely chopped blanched almonds
1 tablespoon kirsch
⅓ cup powdered sugar
1 egg white

FILLING: 2 tablespoons butter
1 egg yolk
1 tablespoon powdered sugar
2 tablespoons cherries, finely chopped

TO DECORATE: unsweetened cocoa powder or grated
semisweet chocolate

In a medium bowl, grate chocolate and mix
with almonds. Add kirsch and sugar.
Gradually add egg white, until mixture binds
well. Form mixture into a log shape. Flatten
to 12″ x 4″.

To make filling, cream butter in a small
bowl. Add egg yolk and sugar; mix well. Stir
in chopped cherries. Spread filling evenly
in a strip along log. Fold over log to enclose
filling. Chill 20 minutes.

To decorate, roll log in cocoa or grated
chocolate to coat the outside. Wrap log in
waxed paper and then in foil; refrigerate. To
serve, cut slices as needed and serve them
very cold. It freezes well and can be cut
frozen, then left to thaw 5 minutes.
Refrigerated it keeps well for 3 weeks,
frozen, 3 months.

Makes 30 pieces.

Christmas Puddings

¾ cup finely chopped dried figs
½ cup ground almonds
2 tablespoons powdered sugar
2 oz semisweet chocolate, grated
2 teaspoons brandy
2 teaspoons lemon juice
1 egg white
TOPPING: 1 tablespoon whipping cream
2 oz white chocolate
1 teaspoon brandy
TO DECORATE: marzipan, page 40, green food coloring, 1 red glacé cherry

In a medium mixing bowl, mix figs, almonds, sugar, semisweet chocolate, brandy and lemon juice. Add egg white, a teaspoon at a time, to bind mixture. Chill 2 hours. Form a small walnut sized ball. Roll in palm of hand until smooth. Using a very sharp knife, cut off ⅓ of ball so ball will sit flat. Repeat, returning extra piece to mixture each time. Refrigerate in a covered container up to 2 weeks.

To make topping, heat cream in a small saucepan until bubbling. Remove from heat and add chocolate. Cover and let stand 5 minutes. Add brandy. Stir until smooth. Trickle topping over each pudding to simulate custard.

To decorate, add green food coloring to marzipan; knead well. Pinch off 40 tiny pieces. Roll each piece into a rectangle. To make leaves, press center of each rectangle and flatten, leaving end as a point. Curve each leaf slightly. Let dry 2 hours. Cut glacé cherry into small pieces. Place 2 leaves on top of each pudding and piece of cherry in center. Refrigerate in a single layer until puddings are firm, or up to 1 week.

Makes 20 puddings.

Nut Snowballs

¼ cup finely ground almonds
¼ cup finely ground hazelnuts
¾ cup powdered sugar
1 egg white

TO COAT: 2 egg whites
powdered sugar

Preheat oven to 350F (180C). Line bottom of baking sheet with waxed paper. In a small bowl, mix nuts together. Add sugar; gradually add sufficient egg white to form a paste.

Wet hands; form nut paste into 24 small round balls. In a small bowl whisk 2 egg whites lightly until slightly frothy. Dip balls into egg whites; roll in powdered sugar to coat.

Place in paper cases on baking sheet and bake 12 to 15 minutes or until golden on top and firm to touch. Remove from baking sheet; cool on a wire rack 12 hours. Dust with a little extra powdered sugar. Store in an airtight container up to 1 week.

Makes 24 snowballs.

Glazed Hazelnut Matchsticks

3 tablespoons hazelnuts
superfine sugar
6 oz puff pastry
ICING: ½ cup powdered sugar
¼ teaspoon lemon juice
½ egg white

Preheat oven to 350F (180C). Roast hazelnuts on a baking sheet 10 minutes or until golden brown and skins are slightly blistered. Wrap nuts in a towel. Let stand 5 minutes. Rub with towel to remove skins. Finely chop nuts. To make icing, in a small bowl, mix powdered sugar and lemon juice. Add egg white, gradually; beat well. Cover tightly and refrigerate 1 hour.

Grease a baking sheet. On a flat surface, generously sprinkled with superfine sugar, roll puff pastry to a very thin 11" x 7" strip. Sprinkle pastry with ⅔ chopped nuts. Fold lengthwise into center. Roll again to a thickness of ½ inch. Place pastry on prepared baking sheet. Cut pastry into 3 long strips; divide strips into ½ inch pieces. Chill for 30 minutes.

Preheat oven to 425F (220C). Stir icing before spreading over the top of each strip. Top with remainder of nuts. Bake in preheated oven 10 minutes or until golden. Adjust oven temperature to 350F (180C). Bake 5 minutes or until center of pastry is cooked. Let stand on baking sheet 1 minute. Carefully cut between strips where icing has joined matchsticks together. Loosen strips from baking sheet. Let stand until completely cold. Cut between matchsticks again. Store matchsticks in an airtight container up to 2 weeks.

Makes about 40 matchsticks.

Marshmallow Nut Fudge

60 marshmallows
⅔ cup butter, cubed
2 tablespoons water
12 oz semisweet chocolate, chopped
1 teaspoon vanilla extract
2½ cups coarsely chopped walnuts

Line bottom of 11″ x 7″ loaf pan with foil. In a medium saucepan, melt marshmallows, butter and water. Stir occasionally. Add chocolate, vanilla and nuts to marshmallow mixture. Stir until evenly mixed and chocolate has melted.

Pour into prepared pan. When cool, refrigerate wrapped in foil.

To serve, cut into 80 pieces.

Makes 80 pieces.

Twice Dipped Strawberries, page 13, make a
refreshing after dinner treat. They can also
be packed prettily and presented as a small
gift or used to decorate rich gâteaux.

A selection of Miniature Tarts: Chocolate
Liqueur Tarts, page 95; Cream Cheese Tarts,
page 94; Lemon Butter Tarts, page 96.

This attractive bunch of grapes is made from
a selection of chocolate trufflles, such as
Almond Praline Truffles, page 30; Orange
Truffles, page 33; Ginger Truffles, page 35;
Cake Truffles, page 36; Almond Prune
Truffles, page 37. Assemble truffles of varying
sizes, fix in place using a little melted
chocolate, pipe chocolate stalks and
decorate with a chocolate leaf.

Clockwise from top: Almond Cookies, page
83; Brandy Snaps, page 88; Chocolate
Almond Crisps, page 91; Orange Buttons,
page 78; Viennese Almond Crescents, page
72; Almond Orange Bread, page 68;
Meringue Crunchies, page 106; Chocolate
Chip Bars, page 75, presented in a box tied
with velvet ribbon and packed in tissue.

An assortment of wafers served with soft
fruits. Clockwise from top: Chocolate
Cinnamon Wafers, page 87; Cigarettes
Russes, page 77; Pistachio Wafers, page 84.

Clockwise from top: Fruit-Filled Chocolate
Cups, page 28; Chocolate-Coated Orange
Strips, page 12; Cherry Nut Chocolates,
page 16; Mocha Coconut Roughs, page 114;
Chocolate-Coated Fruit, page 10; Fruity
Chocolates, page 8; Marzipan Cherry Log,
page 43; Chocolate Marzipan Delights, page
42; Walnut Coffee Creams, page 17;
Chocolate-Coated Fruit, page 10, presented
as a tempting array of fruit, nut and
marzipan confections.

INDEX